PASSING THROUGH THE SHADOWS

HOW FAITH HELPED US PASS THROUGH LIFE-CRUSHING EXPERIENCES

By D. Lee Allison

PRESS

Passing Through Shadows
by D. Lee Allison

Printed in the United States of America

ISBN 1-59781-506-3

Scripture quotations are either from the King James Version or are the author's translation or paraphrase.

www.xulonpress.com

To Joe and Elizabeth
Long-time friends
and fellow-travelers
on the Christian journey.
May God continue to
bless you and yours,
Lee

TABLE OF CONTENTS

INTRODUCTION

I was standing on the mesa of normal living, surveying the horizon of the future. Great plans formed in my mind as I was eagerly anticipating the next step in my life. But life came up behind me and pushed me over the edge into a canyon that I had not seen. Have you experienced that? Your traumatic event may have been betrayal by someone you had trusted implicitly, an economic trauma of major proportions, clinical depression by some family member, an accident that has changed your life forever, a physical change that makes it impossible for you to continue in your accustomed life-style or someone close to you died. My "life-shattering event" was my wife's cancer, her thirteen-year struggle and finally her death.

The book includes stories based on the experiences of real people whose names and a few of the circumstances have been changed to protect their privacy. Conversations have been simulated. Sarah's husband died and she was left with a thirteen-year-old son, Mike, to support. A year later we find her at the bottom of the canyon again because she lost her job without any notice. Jim and Susie fell to the bottom of the spiritual canyon when they received the news that their six-year-old son, Arthur, was diagnosed with Muscular Dystrophy. Isabelle, through a series of excessive stresses, landed in the canyon with clinical depression and thoughts of suicide. Larry landed at the bottom of the canyon troubled with self-doubts and feelings of failure when his wife of twenty years unexpectedly walked out of his life. Michelle was told by her husband Andy to get out. After a number of threats, she realized he meant it and she left with no place to go. We all found ourselves at the bottom of a spiritual canyon bruised and numbed by the fall.

This book is the general description of our spiritual journey out of the canyon to some kind of normalcy after our life-shattering events. I realize that this is necessarily an individual journey so your journey will differ in some of the details from mine and that of my friends. Since I know my story best, it will dominate the others. This is not to imply that my friends' stories are less important. During my struggle with my wife's death sentence and for about five years after her death, I faced a number of problems: shattered dreams, depression, stress, failure and guilt, fear, worry and loss of meaning in my life. By talking with my friends, I find these are common problems. My withered faith begins to take root again and revive when I study the Bible. Therefore, the Bible "stories" are laid along side our stories that are written in the present tense to help you identify with what we went through as we were experiencing it.

This book is written in the hope that it will encourage you who may be struggling to put your life back together. It is my prayer that this description of our struggles will help you to know that others have successfully recovered from a tragic event or series of events.

The first half of the book addresses specific problems that we faced. While fumbling around in the darkness at the bottom of the canyon, we first discover our broken dreams. So the first chapter addresses the disappointment of fading hope and approaching despair. Jesus' disciples found the same thing when they were pushed over the edge by Jesus' death. When examining their journey on the road from Jerusalem to Emmaus, I found parallels between their experience and ours. The next problem we face is denial and I am forced to face the fact of death. My friends face losses also: Sarah, her job; Jim and Susie, the health of their son; Isabelle, her mental health; Larry, his wife and Michelle, her home and family. All of these precipitate a grieving process. The way that Jesus entered in the sorrow of Lazarus' sisters after their brother's death helps relieve some of the numbness that comes as a result of our falls into the canyon.

But then, we wonder: "What's the use? Why try to fight our way back?" Life's meaning is fading fast. In chapter three I look at a way to cope with fading meaning in our lives due to the changes that are drastically altering our life-styles. Then we feel an overwhelming sadness akin to depression. (This chapter is not meant as a substitute for professional help in the case of clinical depression such as the case of Isabelle.) I found that most of us can relate to Elijah's experience and that helps us in our post-trauma blue funk. While groping our way at the bottom of our spiritual canyon, my friends and I find we are not as efficient as we have been. This is accompanied by a sense of failure. Chapter five explains how we are finding help.

Inevitably we find the difficulties of failure are compounded by a sense of guilt as we explore the bottom of the canyon. I asked, "Did I contribute to the cause of this life-changing event? And did my actions cause irreparable damage to someone I love?" My friends are asking similar questions. In chapter six, I try to crack that boulder. In chapter seven, we have to climb over the obstacle of fear. I explain how Isaiah's great statement of the Lord's promise helps clear our vision and bring a little light into our darkness. The last thing we find at the bottom of the canyon is worry. It is hard to deal with. It is a persistent problem. In chapter eight, I look at the Apostle Paul's "formula" for overcoming worry.

The second half of the book discusses some aids in finding the path out of the canyon back to the mesa of emotional stability. Life is not like it was before our falls, but we have healed. There are some things that we found helpful and I share them with you. We start our climb by examining some mistakes that we have made. This helps us to face rationally our part in causing the current difficulties – to accept some of the responsibility for our falls. Following that, we face up to the fact that we are asking the wrong questions. Much of our confusion comes from looking at things from the wrong point of view. Then we look to God's word for strength to fight the battles that have come as a result of these changes that have taken place in our lives. We feel thrown down, but God sets the limits and so we are not destroyed. In spite of the earthen vessel of our human limitations, we find that we have a treasure inside. We may stumble as we head in the wrong direction, but we find strength to get going in the right direction again by the supply of daily grace that God gives us. In the midst of the difficult climb, Jesus promises and gives us peace in the midst of turmoil. There are still some troubling questions that are rather like trying to climb a sheer cliff. I look for help in the writings of the "questioning prophet," Habakkuk. I find some insights that give us the boost that we need, but not the definitive answers that we are seeking.

The monster anger appears. At times my monster was ill-defined — fuzzy. At other times it was well-defined — focused. Some of the others tell me their anger is definitely focused. They are angry with the boss that fired them, the employer that lied to them and contributed to their depression, their "ex" who ran out on them, or their "ex" who ran her out of her own home. As we face and fight with the monster anger, we find a most effective weapon in forgiveness. It really works. Now we are clear to climb over the lip of the mesa. But wait! No sunshine? For a while, we find that we must live under a cloud. At first it is disappointing, but we find that in the long run, it is full of God's grace.

Each chapter begins with a summary (printed in *italics*) that describes briefly the chapter's contents. The rationale behind this is to direct you to the part of the book that is most relevant to the current problems that you are facing. For example, if you are in the process of trying to cope with a sense of anxiety. Should you read the chapter on "Attacking Worry," "Thrown Down But Not Destroyed" or "Peace in Turmoil"? Reading the summaries of these chapters should help clarify the cause of your anxiety or at least give you a clue as to which of these chapters might be of greatest help.

This book goes out to you with a prayer: "May the God of all grace give you wisdom, courage and strength. Wisdom to make the best decisions, the courage to act on those decisions and the strength to successfully move ahead on the spiritual journey of life."

I wish to thank those who encouraged me to have this book published. I am also indebted to the people whose stories I have told. Their patience during our conversations and willingness to answer probing questions allowed me to get a clear picture of their life-crushing experiences and how they were finding the power to cope with them.

PART I

FACING PROBLEMS
SPECIFICALLY
AT THE BOTTOM OF THE
CANYON

CHAPTER 1

COPING WITH BROKEN DREAMS

Summary: *The disciples' dreams of grandeur were shattered by Jesus death. Their concept of the Messiah was too limited in scope. Their grief fogged their vision so that they could not recognize Jesus and receive the truth. However, in the end, their joy was restored by clear vision of reality. I traveled much the same road.*

I seem to be in a dark spiritual canyon. I have fallen. It has been a long fall. Thirteen years of falling, rising, then falling again. Cancer, operations, radiation therapy, remission, cancer, operations, chemotherapy and finally the Cardiac Care Unit. Now I am at the bottom of the canyon — Hattie, my wife, is dead. I am struggling to cope with broken dreams. Is there hope of ever getting beyond this point of darkness? Hope had painted a bright future. I had been eager to get on with life. I was back home after a successful excursion to graduate school. Hattie had a good job. Our children were on their own. Now Hattie and I could go places and do things together. But now that is all in the past. I am alone. Hope seems to be a fragile thing.

Sarah is with me here in the canyon. She grew up in the home of a successful farmer. She married a minister and they had served the church for nearly thirty years. She was a happy mother and homemaker. Life seemed so constant – so dependable. Then she developed a growing premonition – a sense of tragedy. As she was praying one day in July, she sensed a heavy-black veil move toward her to envelop her. She felt like she was being suffocated. Later that day her husband had an accident that left him paralyzed. Three days later, he died. She was left as the sole support of Mike, a thirteen-year-old. She lost her husband. She lost her house, which was furnished by the church. She lost her source of income. There was very little insurance. Her mother and father were dead. "Lord, where do we go from here?" Miraculously, she found a place to live, one room with a shared bathroom and kitchen privileges. She found a job as a switchboard operator for a large industry. Hope was renewed.

"Sarah, why are you back at the bottom of the canyon?" She looks away to hide her tears. "The boss came in this week and said, 'Pack up your things. When you leave this evening, don't come back!'" Her voice drops. "I was fired without any warning. Without a job, I can't pay my rent and I have no place to go." She looks up at the intimidating canyon walls and from her confused and broken heart come sobs quietly asking: "God, where are you?"

The Bible speaks to our situations. Sarah and I move back in time and across the distance to a lonely road from Jerusalem to Emmaus. We see two close friends of Jesus who are shuffling lethargically along the dusty road. The Romans had just executed Jesus, their hope of redemption. We watch and listen. Cleopas sighs: "We had hoped . . ." and his voice trails off. His partner mumbles something. They stumble on. It is obvious that they are near the bottom of the canyon of despair similar to our situation.

"We had hoped!" The tense of the expression, "had hoped" indicates that it is all over. The words are filled with disappointment. They tell of a dream that has been shattered — destroyed. The future is gone. Life sometimes has a way of doing that. The two men are walking from the city of high hopes to their home in the valley of reconsideration. The future that they had planned and hoped for is obviously not to be.

What had they hoped? What dreams have been shattered? They had hoped that this was the One Who would "redeem Israel." (Luke 24:21). With the redemption of Israel would come their liberation from the Romans. Israel would become the dominant world power. They were not alone in their dreams of grandeur. The Scriptures had promised that a king would come and "of the increase of His government . . . there would be no end . . . to establish it." (Isaiah 9:7) Jesus was perfectly qualified to fill the position. Surely, the Messiah had come at last. Long years of answering to foreign governments were about to come to an end. The despised were about to become the despisers. They had mused, "You may laugh at us now, take all our money in taxes, take our coats, force us to carry your soldier's load for a mile but the time is near at hand when the tables will be turned." This Jesus was a miracle worker. Of course He had said, "If you are forced to carry a soldier's load one mile, do a second mile voluntarily." But surely He was just softening them up for the blow that was to come. How clever of Him! Because of Jesus' teaching the Romans would let down their guard and then POW! These disciples could hardly wait. It would be like it used to be in the days of King David. The Golden Age was about to come again.

Judas could hardly wait either. He took matters into his own hands. He apparently figured that he could force Jesus' hand. He had seen Jesus feed five thousand men with just a lad's lunch. No supply-line problems with this Messiah. He had seen Jesus heal the sick and even raise the dead. Suppose a soldier of this King would be so unfortunate as to be injured or even killed in battle. With but a word from Jesus and he would be an able fighter again. No shortage of troops here. Surely Jesus was the one to redeem Israel.

The time was right, too. All those people in Jerusalem celebrating the Passover — a feast commemorating deliverance from Egyptian bondage. Judas seemed to reason that if only he could get Jesus into a situation of direct confrontation with the religious rulers of Israel, He would use His power to bring the "Promised Land" back into the control of the common folks. The ensuing conflict would involve the Romans who would then be subjugated.

Other disciples had similar thoughts. John and James were vying for positions of power in the obviously coming kingdom. Their positions in the inner circle of disciples seemed to insure their success if only they could get to Jesus with the idea before Peter did. Jesus seemed saddened by their request. Maybe He was too busy planning His strategy to bother with such details. This could come later as the new government was being established. In any event, there was an air of expectancy. Something was about to happen.

"But why think about that now? Our dream is dead." For some unknown reason, Jesus had allowed the religious leaders to mock Him, abuse Him both verbally and physically and turn Him over to the Romans for more torture. Finally He was killed — crucified, the death of a criminal of the lowest class. He submitted to all this as a "Lamb" being sheared and then slaughtered. For these disciples, "death" and "the Christ" were not part of the same vocabulary. They had hoped that Jesus was the One Who would redeem Israel. Now He is dead and with Him their dream. "Why had Jesus allowed this? Was He a fake after all? Had we just been suckers?" They couldn't really believe that, but why didn't God perform a miracle — a *Deus ex machina?*

My wife, Hattie, had been diagnosed with Hodgkin's Disease, a cancer of the lymphatic system. After four operations and a regimen of radiation therapy, she was free of cancer. We had been told that if the cancer did not reappear in five years, we were "home free." Every month, then every three months, then every six months we would returned to Birmingham for a check-up. Finally five years passed. At the end of year six, "Come back in a year for a check-up." Wow! A whole year. We were scarred but we were happy again.

At the end of that year we went to Birmingham in a spirit of celebration. We made special plans to go out to eat in some fancy restaurant. But first the check-up. Hattie went for her x-ray. When she came out to the waiting room I knew that something had gone wrong. She said to me, "Dr. Radiologist wants to talk to both of us in his office." My confidence evaporated. My fears revived. The celebration collapsed. The doctor threw the x-ray up onto the viewer and pointed to a shadow. He explained: "This may be a lesion or scar tissue from the previous surgery but we need to go in a have a first-hand look at it. We need your permission." After Hattie and I discussed the situation in private, we decided that it would be best to allow the surgery even though it meant opening up her chest again.

The surgery was scheduled. The day came. Once more I found myself in the "Day of Surgery" waiting room alone — Well, not really alone because other families filled the room. None of our children was able to come. So I sat alone with my book. Noon came. I was not hungry. The phone rang again. This time it was for me. The surgeon wanted to talk to me. We met in a private place and he explained: "The cancer (there was that 'C' word again!) was wrapped around the nerve (not another nerve) that controls a portion of the left side of the diaphragm. I decided to sacrifice the nerve. I believe that I got it all."

"Will any further treatment be required or recommended?"

"That will be up to Dr. Oncologist."

Chemotherapy and nausea, baldness and wigs, good days and bad, pain and suffering, temporary paralysis and temporary recovery. Life returned to a sad routine. In spite of all this, Hattie continued to work at TVA. Finally after a year, Hattie decided to retire. That provided some relief.

But now for more than two months, she had been bedfast and in and out of the hospital. Following that, she lay in CCU for nearly a month. At first she was paralyzed from the neck down and then gradually began to get some movement and feeling back into her body. Hope revived. We prayed for a miracle. Our pastor prayed for a miracle. The church prayed for a miracle. Many of the faculty and students at the university prayed for a miracle.

Friends and relatives all over the country prayed for a miracle. Even strangers, when they heard of our circumstances, said that they would pray for a miracle. There were no geographical or denominational boundaries. Hundreds of people united in one petition: "Heal Hattie." But she died.

Sarah had been praising God for His goodness. In spite of her losses, God had provided a place to stay and a good job to pay for it. The future was back! Her husband was still dead but God was helping her heal. Mike's school problems were being solved. She and Mike had bonded at a deeper level. Now this!

Were Sarah and I blinded by circumstances? Was there a bigger picture that we were not aware of?

Now back to the journey. As the two friends are tossing their doubts back and forth another man joins them. He seems to be ignorant of the things that have spelled an end to their plans. It is Jesus but these disciples are so caught up in their own thoughts and disillusionment that they do not recognize their risen Lord. Grief has a way of drugging us. It will distort the picture and disguise the truth. It is emotional and not rational. The mind cannot control it. Grief temporarily blinds. It had distorted their concept of God.

This is happening to me. I have trouble making any sense out of what is happening. I am tired of playing games. Any time God wants to, I am ready to welcome Hattie back. Some of the events in the three months preceding Hattie's death seem like cruel jokes. My view of Christ has become distorted. I cannot recognize Him.

Sarah, too, is blinded by grief over her new circumstances. Losing her husband was bad enough. Her faith had been shaken but it had been partially restored and hope had been renewed when she found work so easily. Her living quarters were cramped and left much to be desired — true — but at least it was a roof over their heads. But now that is apparently in the past. Hope is gasping. Her Lord cannot be seen because of the shadows. Is He even there?

Grief, disillusionment and disappointment write across our consciousness in such bold face print that we can see nothing good. Shattered dreams leave room for only negative thoughts. These disciples could see only the negatives. Initially, in reporting the events to the stranger they tried to related what they had seen. Then they added a fact to the account that did not mean anything to them because of their negative mood. They said that some women had visited the tomb that morning and found it empty. "How do you explain that? Why bother? It would probably only add to the confusion."

I find it natural to think only of the loss since my wife's death. I have been in no mood to think about what I have left and of the friends that are helping me at this difficult time. Likewise, Sarah is mentally fogged-in. We are trying to fit the facts into the pattern of our presuppositions. This wrecks our objectivity. We distort the truth and lose our view of the whole picture.

The result of these staggering blows is a battered faith. Confusion is the order of the day. What do I really believe? I am not sure. Do I really believe in life as a conscious existence after death? Before it became so important, I would have readily said "Yes!" Shortly after Hattie's death, I must honestly answer, "I don't know." In all my Christian experience I have never been so uncertain and confused. When my father died, I had a deep sense of well being. I was confident that he was not dead. There was grief. I cried. But even in the pain of separation there was the assurance that I would see him again and that he was alive in a new dimension. My wife is dead and I have none of this. There is just a void with nagging questions about her condition or even if she still exists. It is pure torture. Will I ever dream again? If I do, the reconstructed dream will not be the same. Could there be reason to hope again?

As these disciples are traveling with this "stranger," I hear Him leading them step by step to a clear vision of reality. As a first step, Jesus is asking them to relate the facts as objectively as possible. They cannot blur over the events by saying , "the things which were come to pass. . ." Jesus wanted to know "What things?" They recite the facts:

- Jesus was a prophet mighty in deed and word.
- The chief priests and rulers delivered him to death.
- He was crucified three days ago
- They once had believed that Jesus was the Christ.
- Some women of the group found the tomb empty.
- The women claimed to have seen angels who said that Jesus was alive.

The facts are both positive and negative.

Sarah and I take this first step. Sarah states:

- My husband is dead
- I lost my job without warning
- I must move from this expensive room with kitchen privileges
- Mike and I are healthy
- Mike and I have bonded — we're in this together
- We live in a city small enough to be safe but large enough for opportunity
- We have a caring community in the church

The facts are both positive and negative.

Now it's my turn:

- Hattie is dead
- My children are alive but in distant cities
- I still have my Ph.D.
- I am still Head of the Department of Physics and Earth Science
- My faculty, staff and students are supportive
- I have a caring community in the church

The facts are both positive and negative.

Then Jesus tells that these disciples that they are "slow of heart to believe." (Luke 24:25). As we listen we hear that their preconception of the Christ limited their view of redemption. Their prejudice made the Scripture say what they wanted to hear. It seems that He is about to cure this by His exposition of the Scriptures. He shows them that God's definition of "redeem" does not correspond with theirs. God's view is long range instead of short range. He sees things from the panorama of eternity instead of time. He is interested in treating the disease, sin, instead of the symptoms, political bondage.

Their plans are too small in scope. What they are thinking of as redemption is on the human level, the horizontal plane. They are thinking only of their present position and misery. They fail to see God's broader plan that includes another dimension. Their plan is only a temporary solution to the problem. In formulating their dream they had bleeped over the "Suffering Servant" passages. "He is despised and rejected of men, a man of sorrows and acquainted with grief. . . He is brought as a lamb to the slaughter and as a sheep before her shearers is dumb, so he opened not his mouth." (Isaiah 53:3,7) Sin has entered God's creation and brought with it destruction, bondage, and misery. God's redemption means that the Son of God, Who was in the flesh, was "wounded for our transgressions, bruised for our iniquities, the chastisement of our peace was upon him and with his stripes we are healed." (Isaiah 53:5) (For us living in this century, we can thank God that He did not accept the disciple's idea of redemption.) Jesus asks, "Ought not Christ to have suffered these things and to enter into his glory?" (Luke 24:26). As Jesus expounds the Scriptures to them, their faith was being renewed and their hearts once more glow with the warmth and love of a faith begotten of God.

My idea of a healing was for Hattie to be physically restored. I looked for evidence. There was none. I only observed her getting progressively worse and losing more and more control over her body. I should have been prepared for her death but my preconceived idea about what God would do kept the whole truth from me. My idea of healing short-range. God's idea of healing was long-range. Hattie's primary doctor had been called by other members of the staff a "pathological optimist." On the Sunday before Hattie died on Tuesday, he indicated that he was afraid that we were going to lose the battle for her life. At that time I said to him, "I have prayed that God would heal Hattie and maybe this is His answer." He studied that for a while and then responded sadly, "Maybe so. There is a good chance that she would never walk again even if she recovered." Our plans were too small in scope. What we wanted was to have Hattie physically healed and able to fully participate in our lives again as she had in the past — the "Good Old Days" restored. At best, this would have been a temporary solution because sooner or later she would die. God saw that the best solution was to heal her permanently at this time.

I am bringing my doubts to the Bible for exposure. In the light of God's Word, I am trying to read God's Word for what it says and not what I want it to say. By the help of the Holy Spirit, I am confident that I will have my heart healed and my positive faith restored.

How much faster the journey went after this stranger had joined them! As they are arriving at home, they must invite their newfound friend in to eat with them. He must spend the night with them. It might be inconvenient but the spiritual was becoming more important than the material. This guest had fed their souls. The least the disciples could do was take care of some of "this stranger's" physical needs even if it meant a bit of extra work on their part. Now comes the biggest surprise of all! Jesus is indeed alive. By a great leap of faith, their eyes are opened and they see Jesus who had been there all the time. The familiar function of the blessing and breaking of the bread — this tie to the past — was the necessary gentle nudge to awaken the eyes of their soul. Then He vanished out of their sight. Just as Jesus had warned Mary Magdalene in the garden that they could not fall into the old patterns of their former relationship, just so here He is, by His actions, indicating that this is a new era. They had to share the good news. They immediately headed back to Jerusalem to tell their friends that Jesus is alive. But Jesus is no longer limited by space and time. He is in Emmaus with them. He vanishes. Before they know it, He is talking to Peter in private reconciliation. When they arrive back at Jerusalem, He reveals Himself again. Christ had conquered death.

He has promised that we shall live also. Death is not a period at the end of the sentence of life. The grave is open at both ends. There is life after physical death. Hattie lives in my past. I am continually reminded of her by things that she has done for me. When I iron my shirt in the morning, I think of her. She always insisted that I look "nice". She also lives in the lives of our children. What a wonderful legacy she has left me in them. Yet I believe that she has entered into a new relationship with her Lord — alive in a way that is beyond imagination. After she became paralyzed by a stroke, her mind was clear and we could communicate by reading her lips. She said that during the ordeal of being put on machines and having a series of tests run, she tried to think of the twenty third Psalm. She continued, "It became clear." She and I then repeated the Psalm together. Surely this Great Shepherd has led her "through the valley of the shadow of death" to the blessed pasture on the other side. My dreams are changing. They are being rebuilt with the things that remain and in hope based on a rejuvenated faith. I feel a little better now.

In light of this new point of view, Sarah is reevaluating her situation. Instead of looking only at what she has lost, she now realizes that she has much to be thankful for. True, she is still unemployed. The self-devastating firing has damaged her feeling of self-worth. However, she still has her health. The fact that she is responsible for Mike gives her some reason to go on — gives her some meaning in life. With this new outlook, she now has energy to look expectantly to the future.

Oh, we have more company. I hope that our examination of broken dreams will help you to dream again.

CHAPTER 2

DEALING WITH DEATH

Summary: *We pray for healing and our loved one dies. We must face the reality of death. This is a real test of our faith. If we will let Him, Jesus will enter into our grief, temper the test and help us realize that death puts life in proper perspective.*

One of the big problems for me at the bottom of the canyon into which I have fallen is facing the reality of my wife's death. It's true that Sarah had to deal with this a year ago but now she is dealing with another problem — a feeling of abandonment by God.

When I wake up in the morning, my wife is no longer with me. I have a strong urge to call the hospital. Then I remember she is gone. My heart is stabbed again. "Tragedy, such as death, is something that happens to other people — far away. It surely can't be happening to me or mine. A friend or close relative of mine experience a life-changing event? Get real! That just doesn't happen to us." Our experience of denial is not unique. In crises, large or small, the first reaction is to assume that it really didn't happen. All of us at the bottom of the canyon are in the daze of unreality. "It really didn't happen." But bottom of this canyon is no place to stay. Since we are here let's work together to face all our problems and eventually find our way back up to the mesa. I will try to share with you some of the things that we are learning. We are finding help in the Bible.

This recorded incident is helping me. Jesus and His friends were on vacation far away from the sometimes-admiring and sometimes-angry crowds and the powerful enemies that were calling for His head. As He relaxed, a friendly runner rushed up with the bad news that His friend Lazarus was quite ill. Lazarus' sisters requested that Jesus come at once. Jesus dismissed the runner, told him thanks for the message and that He would take care of the problem. Two days later, Jesus said to His friends, "Well, vacation is over. I must go back and awaken Lazarus."

Jesus was referring to Lazarus's death. Jesus had tried to use this common euphemism but the disciples refused to believe that death had claimed this friend of Jesus. Had not Jesus said that this illness was not unto death? It was natural that when He now said that Lazarus was asleep that was a good sign. To think that Lazarus was dead would be the same as accusing Jesus of failing. So, Jesus said bluntly, "Lazarus is dead!" (John 11:14).

I am finding that there is a reluctance to talk about death. When my wife, Hattie, died, my daughter Janet and I were alone in the waiting room of the Cardiac Care Unit. The attending physician and the nurse that had been with Hattie when she died came to the door of the waiting room and just stood and looked at us. They could not bring themselves to say, "Your wife and mother is dead." I believe that there are possibly four reasons for this. They had fought too hard for a month to keep her alive, and thus they hated to admit defeat. They had learned to love her during the time they cared for her and it hurt too much for them to say that that relationship was at an end. When a relationship is severed, grieving takes place. Further, to say, "Your wife is dead" was to face up to their own mortality and that generally makes people uncomfortable. Finally, there was no way of predicting our reaction to the announcement.

All of us must deal with death sometime. Since this is my

current problem, I am going to try to reconstruct the incidents surrounding Lazarus' death. The details of Lazarus' illness are not given because our reporter was with Jesus, about twenty miles away. With the help of our imagination, we will construct an "it might have been" scenario based on the facts available. Perhaps Lazarus developed a headache but didn't mention it. His oldest sister, Martha, who felt responsible for keeping the household humming, sensed that something was wrong. After about a day, it seemed safe to mention it. She asked him what was the trouble. By this time he was feverish. As the hours passed, he became obviously worse. "Maybe we ought to let Jesus know. He would surely do something." They were still reluctant to bother their Friend. Lazarus' condition continued to worsen. Finally, when they couldn't get the fever down, they sent a runner with the message: "The one whom You love is sick." Surely that would bring Jesus or at least he would speak the word and heal their brother as He had the centurion's servant. Unfortunately, by the time the runner found Jesus and gave Him the message, Lazarus was already dead.

The death of a loved one tests our faith. Had Jesus forsaken His friends? So it seemed. In seeking for an answer to that question they might have remembered that the last time Jesus was in their area, an angry mob tried to stone Him. Maybe it wasn't safe for Him to come back. But then He had performed a healing at a distance before, why not this time? When Jesus did show up both Mary and Martha stated their sadly tested faith: "If You had been here, my brother would not have died." Martha's faith still showed some life in "God will give You whatever You ask."

I am finding it easy to question myself into a corner. When Hattie was paralyzed in the hospital, I wondered why. She had been a fine Christian for at least forty years. In recent years, it seemed the more she suffered, the more she loved and thought of others. For example, she lay paralyzed in the CCU of the UAB hospital on Easter Sunday morning. When my son and I arrived, she insisted that we find a store open and purchase some candy for the nurses. She wouldn't let us wait until Monday!

Why should being paralyzed be added to her already difficult burden? Perhaps Jesus would get glory to His name by healing her completely. "Lord, one whom you love is desperately ill. Won't You come and touch her?" He allowed her to die! Some had boldly expressed confidence that Christ would heal Hattie. Now we are all left to try to explain why she died.

From the report of John, we find that instead of forsaking His friends, Jesus was praying for them. This is indicated (John 11:41) when He prayed, "I thank You that You have heard me. . . ." It appears that Jesus had been praying about this for some time while He seemed so far away.

Jesus was "beyond Jordan" when word came about the illness of his friend. The disciples immediately went into a huddle. They were happy to hear that "this sickness is not unto death" because that allowed them to escape from the dilemma that was the subject of their huddle: return and be killed, or stay hidden and betray our friends. They breathed a sigh of relief. But what did Jesus mean that it was "for the glory of God, that the Son of God might be glorified thereby?" (John 11:4). Jesus seemed to be spending an unusual amount of time in prayer. Two days later the startling announcement came: "Lazarus is dead." A real test of their faith.

Since the disciples were not so close to Lazarus emotionally as his sisters, Jesus could reason with them about the situation. When they began to discuss the situation, it seemed logical that they would stay where they were. Since Lazarus was dead, why go back to face the embarrassment of being late. (They evidently had forgotten about Jairus' daughter who came back to life at the command of Jesus.) Besides there was a danger of Jesus being killed by His enemies should He return to Bethany. Why should He risk His life for someone who is already dead? In the face of this test, Jesus addresses the issue with: "Are there not twelve hours in a day? If anyone walks in the day, he stumbles not because he sees the light of this world. But if a man walks in the night, he stumbles because there is no light in him." (John 11:9-

10). Jesus is dealing with death here by a rational explanation. The death they feared was His. He indicated that He could not be killed until His day's work was complete. The argument was only partially successful. The disciples decided to cast their lot with Him and if need be to die with Him.

In dealing with Martha, His approach was suited to the extraverted personality of His friend. Martha was a doer. Even her grief was expressed in action. From the account of the two sisters in Luke we can see Martha scurrying around to fix food, clear up and wash the dirty dishes. After all, these guests that came to help them mourn must be taken care of. Then there were times that she needed fresh air. Just to walk in fact of the open. Anything to keep her mind from addressing the nagging questions about "why?" and facing the the death of her brother. On one of these walks, she went again to the village limits and looked in the direction of the Jordan. This time she saw a small group. There was something familiar about the leading figure. Jesus had come at last. Her heart jumped with hope and then plunged into distress. The roller coaster emotions characteristic of the recently bereaved were evident. She had so longed for His coming and now that it was about to become a reality she was almost afraid. She had been disappointed when He had tarried. Now what could she hope for? She approached Him with a weakened faith. He did not scold her for not trusting Him fully. He talked with her gently and endeavored to rebuild the faith that had been buffeted by misunderstanding. When Martha needed some time to ponder what Jesus had just said, He asked her to call Mary.

Mary was introverted. She thought deep thoughts. She loved to listen to Jesus as He awakened inspiration in her soul. As He talked, she saw the world from a different perspective. Surely He was not strictly of this world. But now her heart was broken. Her brother had died and Jesus didn't seem to care. She wanted to be alone. "Why must these pesky 'mourners' hang around?" she wondered. When she sought solace at the tomb, they followed her there. There was no place for her to grieve in private. When Jesus came, her heart knew that He would at least understand. Understand he did. She greeted Him with the same statement that Martha had used, but with an attitude of worship which was characteristic of Mary. Jesus' response was appropriate. He joined her in her grief. He wept. Not just quietly and surreptitiously wiping a tear but was visibly moved to grief with this sorrowing woman.

By His tears, Jesus was endorsing this natural expression of bereavement. I, like Mary, wept without shame when my wife died. There was no feeling of guilt. Grief is natural. You, too, should feel free to express your genuine grief by whatever means is appropriate for your personality. Don't be afraid of what others might think. However, grief is not rational. It does no good to reason with someone like Mary. (I find no comfort in trying to reason with myself.) Jesus knew this and entered into her grief rather than scolding her for her broken heart. Some well-meaning people will chatter on about "God's will" and our acceptance of our trauma as being for "the best" or worse, spout fatalistic platitudes while the broken heart still bleeds and looks for some place to escape. Jesus tears reached out to Mary in a way that no words could express.

After my wife's death, a friend of mine came down from Nashville and we went to lunch together. Over our lunch we talked about my wife's illness and death and about my friend's recent divorce. We cried together, quietly sharing at a level that was too deep for words. It was this kind of love that Jesus expressed as Mary wept and worshiped.

I ask myself, "Why I am crying?" I suppose it sounds like a silly question if you haven't been there. Small things trigger a crying spell since my wife's death. Often it is most unexpected. Enter a shopping mall, remember how she liked to shop, pass a dress shop or shoe store and I can stand it no longer. A visit to Niagara Falls and here I go again. Why do I cry? In all honesty, I can say that I do not believe the reason is self-pity. We had loved deeply. Now part of me is missing. Where is she now? I don't believe that she is in the grave. Our love was too enduring to be destroyed by death, but for me, crying was a natural expression of my sorrow. On one occasion I expressed my feelings this way:

> Oh love, maker of pain,
> Thou hast strangled my heart
> Weaving my life into the warp and woof of another
> And now she is gone and my life is in shreds.

I can identify with Mary, but will not argue with those who are more like Martha. The wonderful thing about it is that Jesus treats us in our grief in the way best suited to our personalities. On the other hand, Sarah identifies with Martha. When her husband died, she had about a month to start life over. She was responsible for arranging for her husband's funeral and burial. While her husband was alive, he would read a magazine, see an article that might make a good illustration for a sermon, mark the article with the intent of filing it away. Instead of completing the task, he would throw the magazine onto the growing pile to be dissected later. Now Sarah had all this to dispose. Then there were his books – which ones to keep for her personal library, which ones to save for Mike and which ones to give away. She had to find a place to live. She had to move. She had to clean up the present house and possibly store her furniture. She had get Mike situated in a new school. She had to find a job. Mike never saw her cry. She didn't have time to cry. She was busy "doing" instead of "feeling."

Just so, at this time Sarah is feeling vulnerable and I am finding that grief involves a certain amount of anxiety about my own physical mortality. Jesus faced the fact that by raising Lazarus He was sealing His own doom. He knew that when word of what He was about to do for His friends in Bethany reached the chief priests that they would plot to kill Him. It must have passed through His mind that Mary, who was so broken hearted about her brother, would have her faith severely tried by what would transpire shortly. His tears mingled with hers because all too soon, He would join the ranks of the dead and Mary would once again be bereft; apparently left without a Comforter. After Jesus' death, things would be different. The end of a loving relationship was in sight.

Jesus did not scold Mary or Martha about the "if only's" that they both expressed. After a loved one dies or a relationship is severed, there are always thoughts about what would have happened "if". It is not wise to linger in the valley of the "if only's", but Jesus allowed them to visit there without allowing them to stay. "If only You had been here" to which He responded implicitly, "I wasn't so let us see where we can go from here."

I thank the Lord for tempering Hattie's death for me. I have no regrets, thanks to the way God worked things out. My wife had returned home from the hospital on Tuesday. She was unable to get out of bed. Friday night she experienced a period of extreme weakness that lasted about half an hour. After a second one, I suggested that I call the ambulance to take her back to the hospital. She objected. The next time she felt worse and agreed that I call the doctor. By this time it was Saturday morning. After talking with the doctor, we arranged for her to be transported to the hospital by a special ambulance sent from Birmingham. She was admitted to CCU and watched carefully. About five o'clock Sunday morning she had a stroke, stopped breathing, and nearly went into cardiac arrest. Had she been at home, I could not have revived her, and might even have found her dead in bed. Following her stroke, she had the best care that money could buy. In addition, she was attended by the most loving group of nurses and doctors that I have ever met. I still hurt when I realize that I have lost her, but thank God, I don't have to dwell in the valley of the "if only's".

When I face up to the fact that Hattie is dead, really dead, it helps me see my life through a new perspective. Such a trauma is a time for re-evaluation. As things move on at the normal pace and about the same level, I tend to be lulled into thinking that life consists of getting up in the morning, performing my job during the day, eating supper in the evening, and going to bed at night.

Repeat the cycle. It is like being on a luxury liner on a voyage across the ocean. By the daily routine of relaxation and entertainment we tend to forget that we are traveling. Life is a journey. Daily routine is not permanent. We are creatures of time and eternity. Broken relationships make us face the facts.

When Jesus returned four days after Lazarus' death, he made a startling claim to Martha. "I am the resurrection and the life, he that believes in me, though he were dead, yet shall he live. Whoever lives and believes in me will never die." (John 11:25). At first glance these claims seem to be contradictory. How could a man "live even though he dies?" Jesus is trying to help His friends put life in a proper perspective. There is physical existence called life. There is death that ends this aspect of life. There is life that is not dependent on the physical. A person is more than a body. The body is limited by time and space. The life that Jesus talks about in the phrase "Whoever is alive . . ." is eternal life — life in another dimension.

After Martha had time to wonder about the things that Jesus said in the light of the current state of her belief, Jesus decided that it was time for some evidence. Facts that would give credence to His claims. He asked to visit the grave. They complied with His request and there He continued to show His emotions. To help his followers to see life in a new light, He asked that the stone be removed. Martha wasn't ready for that. "But Lord, he has been dead four days! Surely You know that by now the spirit is hopelessly separated from the body and his body is decomposing badly." Upon Jesus' insistence they removed the stone. Then Jesus revealed His heart in thanking God for answering His prayer. He, Who claimed to be the resurrection and the life, gave evidence of that in the physical realm. He called to Lazarus and Lazarus came back from death even after he had been dead four days. By this act Jesus sought their trust in the realm of the spiritual also. He is "the resurrection and the life."

It is my observation that in our journey through the ups and downs of life there is one ultimate reality — death. Most of us will experience the death of someone who is emotionally close to us like Sarah and I have. We don't like to think about it. Even though we would not choose it, it will be thrust upon us. When it is, I am finding help in the fact that Jesus loves me and is tempering the blow to help me in this time of faith-shaking crisis. I accept His love and realize His concern for all of us as His children. After the initial shock of realizing what has happened, He is helping me to put my life back together with a better sense of what is important and real compared to the trivial and ephemeral. At least it is helping me to enter into the experience of Mary (and Martha).

CHAPTER 3

SURVIVING WHEN LIFE'S MEANING FADES

Summary: We meet Jim and Susie and consider their problem. We all build a worldview from little pieces of our experience fit into a framework that we then accept as foundational. This gives life meaning. Relationships also contribute to meaning in our lives. When something happens that doesn't seem to fit our worldview or disrupts our relationships, our lives are shattered. Trust in God and trust in Jesus will help us keep our perspective and put our lives back together.

In the darkness of our souls at the bottom of the canyon, questions about the meaning of life are beginning to demand our attention. You may be having the same problem.

Sarah is struggling with a problem of self-worth. Losing her husband had made no sense. During the year that followed, however, she realized that she was developing in areas that she would not have if her husband had lived. But now this? Losing her job really makes no sense at all. How could this fit into life's meaning?

Before Hattie's sickness, life had the usual ebb and flow but on the whole it was good. I had been a Christian for many years

37

and had a good relationship with God that gave my life meaning. As a family, we enjoyed the blessings of our loving heavenly Father. Oh, I had read about others who had been deprived of the means of pursuing their life's goals — For example, Joni Eareckson (now Tada) who became a quadriplegic at age seventeen. But that was not for me. I had carefully constructed my worldview from little pieces of experience that seemed to fit into a pattern. Now at the bottom of my spiritual canyon, everything that gave meaning to my life seems to be fading. This does not match my expectations. I am becoming disillusioned. I am joined by Jim and Susie. Let me tell their story.

Jim and Susie sat near each other in study hall their senior year in high school. They would do things to pester each other but that was in fun. They were just friends and not especially attracted to each other. However, after they graduated and had gone their separate ways, they thought of each other, made contact, started to date and finally, after many months, were married. It was a good match. They were happy together. Three years after they were married, Arthur was born. They were ecstatic. He was a delight. No problems.

But later, even though he was fifteen-months-old, he still had not taken his first step. They noticed when they put him down on the floor and helped him stand that his feet were badly splayed. As parents, they expressed their concerns to the doctor. The doctor examined Arthur and decided that his hip structure was abnormal. He recommended corrective braces. With the aid of the braces, Arthur soon began to walk. He continued developing. Later, he improved enough to have his braces removed. He was a good-natured little boy. He bonded with both of his parents. As he became more mobile, he remained unusually clumsy and his way of walking might be described as a waddle. When Arthur was three, Ken was born. As they grew older, Arthur and Ken became inseparable. Arthur still stumbled frequently. Ken soon was more coordinated than he.

Jim and Susie noticed the difference in the development of

their boys. Which one was normal? When Arthur was six, they concluded that Ken's physical development was normal. They decided that Arthur's problem was something more serious than a skeletal structure. They prayed for help. Although they wanted a definite diagnosis so that the problem could be corrected, they wanted to stay optimistic. "We will see a specialist, he will diagnose and treat the problem and then Arthur will soon be as coordinated as Ken."

They were referred to a specialist in a city about one hundred miles east of home. With the aid of many x-rays and other tests, the doctor mapped Arthur's skeleton. There was nothing wrong with his bone structure. That's the good news. The specialist gave them a sealed envelope to deliver to their pediatrician. Is there bad news in the envelope? Half-way home they could stand the suspense no longer. They pulled off the road, stopped, tore open the envelope and read the diagnosis – Muscular Dystrophy. Prognosis – maybe six years to live. They were devastated. How could God do this to them?

Jim grew up embracing the faith of his family. Susie was of a different faith. Before they were married, Jim became convinced of the validity of Susie's faith and was converted. Susie's parents, Ben and Betty, are supportive as Jim and Susie struggle to make sense out of this tragedy. Jim's family remains aloof supposing that it is Jim's punishment for his conversion. In searching for meaning, Jim and Susie are seeking answers. They believe that God is good and also knows all things. "Since He knew that Arthur would be born with this disease, why wasn't he still-born or naturally aborted? Or better yet, why was he conceived? Why does someone we love so much have to suffer? Is God testing our faith and when we have passed the test does He plan to heal Arthur?"

Recently Susie met a single-mom whose son has Muscular Dystrophy. When the child was diagnosed, his father left — "After all this is passed on through the mother's bloodline and so it was her problem!" Susie had a disturbing thought. "Will Jim desert me and leave me to deal with this by myself? But Jim isn't that kind of a man. Our relationship is really solid and meaningful. We love each other too much to let this come between us. But then . . .?" — When Jim arrived home he detected that Susie was upset. "What is wrong, dear?" At first Susie was quiet. Then she blurted out: "You aren't about to leave me, are you?" Jim wondered, "Where did that come from!?" Then tearfully she spilled out whole story. Jim took her gently in his arms and said with conviction: "Susie, we are in this together. It is not your fault any more than it is mine. Arthur is a special child. God has given him to both of us. Assuredly, God is merciful and will give us grace sufficient for our need. Let's pray together."

Arthur started to school. The only way that he could maneuver the steps to the entrance was to crawl up the steps. Some of the other children watched him and started to laugh. This was the beginning and he has become the butt of other children's pranks. For example, he has some trouble walking and the other children love to trip him to see if they could make him fall. Jim and Susie are tempted to take him out of school. They want to shelter him from abuse. On the other hand, they want him to lead as normal a life as possible. There is clearly nothing wrong with his mind. Their worldview is confused. What does all this mean? When the principal became aware of Arthur's problem, he arranged for him to be transferred to a school where there were no intimidating steps at the entrance. Thank God, they are not fighting this alone but there are still questions. The big one is "why?"

So as a group, we are looking to the Bible for help. As we read the Bible, we use our imagination to go back to a time and place in Galilee where we meet a man named John. His earliest recollection was of a particular event. His mother directed the servants as they thoroughly cleaned the house especially looking to rid the house of something called "leaven". At the same time John was being prepared by special training to take part in something which had an aura of excitement about it. After a meal that tasted different from the usual fare, at the appropriate time he, as the youngest lad allowed at the table, arose and recited the question that he had been taught: "What is the meaning of all these services?" This was the first time that he really listened as his father recited the long and illustrious history of the great nation Israel. Zebedee told of the first Passover, the subsequent flight from Egypt, the entrance to the "Promised Land", and then of the "Golden Years" of David. Little John's heart swelled with pride that he was somebody. Because of his heritage, he felt really important.

From the time he could talk, his parents helped him to memorize many prayers and sacred sayings. At age six, he entered the primary school associated with the synagogue. There the emphasis was upon reading and memorizing the Scriptures. He also was required to learn a trade. "He who does not teach his son a trade, teaches him to be a thief!" As soon as he was strong enough, he went with his father and older brother down to the Sea of Galilee to fish. He learned to cast the net, to draw the net, to cull and sort the fish and to mend and store the nets. This, too, played an important part in his developing philosophy of life.

Another incident is vividly recalled as he tells us of his first visit to Jerusalem. At first glimpse of the temple as a twelve-year-old, he thought that his heart would stop because of the awesome sight. The golden roof, the tiered courtyard, the priests in the most ornate clothing that John had ever seen, the pungent smoke of the sacrifice. If this was representative of where God meets His people, God must be an awe-inspiring Being. Later he associated the word "holy" with this feeling.

At this early age, John began to develop certain mystical qualities. He realized that, although there were solid things, such as fishing equipment, there was also another aspect of the world that was just as real — maybe even more so. When he thought about God, there came to him a sense that he was dealing with the Ultimate Reality. Life had more significance than what he ate, where he slept, and the kind of clothes he wore. The future became important as it found its roots in the past. The great King

David would someday be superseded by another. The "Golden Age" of the past was but a shadow of what lay in the future. Perhaps all these strange feelings would some day congeal into a working philosophy of life.

When John became a man, with most of his formal training in the distant past, he worked the business with his family and enjoyed his trips to Jerusalem to peddle fish products. Still, every time he saw the temple there was a strange feeling that there were fundamental conflicts in what he interpreted as life's meaning. Surely there was more to life than fish. Then one day while he was back in Galilee, Jesus came by while he and his brother, James, were mending their nets and made a statement that began to clear up this ambiguity of life. He said, "Follow me, and I will make you fishers of men."

As he became Jesus' constant companion, John began to see some of the relationship between the physical and spiritual worlds. Two incidents will illustrate how this understanding developed. On one occasion they were in Peter's house. The crowd was large. Dust and small debris began to fall near where Jesus stood and when they looked up, they saw a growing hole in the roof. Soon a man was let down on his pallet until he was about level with Jesus waist. At this point, Jesus looked up into the four grinning faces of the men who were holding the ropes and then back to the paralyzed man on the pallet. He said to the paralytic, "Your sins are forgiven." The man smiled, obviously happy for the first time in quite a while, but Jesus statement brought a whisper of criticism among the Pharisees that were present. Jesus then asked, "Is it easier to say 'Your sins are forgiven' or 'Get up and walk', but lest you doubt my authority to forgive sins" He turned to the sick man and continued, "Get up and walk!" Jesus seemed to be saying that the most important things about life were those invisible things about us that are associated with our relation to God. The visible things were used by Jesus to teach us about the real things in life.

The other incident took place north of the Sea of Galilee.

Jesus had drawn the attention of a large crowd, as usual, and he had kept them past time to eat. Then with just five barley pancakes and two sardines, a lad's lunch that a boy had donated, Jesus fed five thousand men and whatever women and children were there. A miracle indeed! Once again the physical needs of men had surfaced. Was there a spiritual lesson to be learned here? Jesus said, "I am the Bread of life which came from heaven to be with you." Most interesting!

In spite of the many spiritual lessons that John and the others were being exposed to, as the initial excitement wore off and the routine of life with its demands settled in, the meaning of life, which formed their foundation for actions, became sublimated and thus subconscious. False concepts developed. Lulled by the routine, John assumed that the present relationship that he had with Jesus would last forever.

We know because we fell into the same trap. I subconsciously thought that Hattie, my wife, was physically immortal - that she would be with me here on earth forever. Sarah had thought that her job was secure. Had not her job been a gift from God? Until the diagnosis, Jim and Susie thought that Arthur was a healthy child.

Another way of thinking about that, my perspective about life and its significance became blurred by the here and now. Every day I would get up, eat breakfast, go to work, come home and be greeted by a smile and a kiss. I was loved and I knew it. Hattie trusted me and I trusted her. She was consistent and I grew to depend upon her. This security gave meaning to life.

Sarah also would get up, get breakfast for Mike, take the bus to work, come home, ask Mike how his day was at school, go to bed and repeat the process. Life made sense again.

Jim and Susie would wake up, Jim would go to his work while Susie would feed and bathe Arthur, play with him while he responded with a smile. Then later when Jim came home, they fell into an evening routine that gave a sense stability. As Arthur grew older, Susie went back to work. Susie's mother took care of

Arthur when his parents were at work. Everything was quite normal. This routine seems permanent. Life was good.

John evidently developed much the same attitude. Jesus was nearly always around. Oh true, occasionally they would miss Him early in the morning and when they would hunt Him down they would find Him praying. But John and his friends ate together, walked together, talked together and shared the secure love of Jesus.

Another thing that we have observed from this new perspective is that we anticipated the future based on the pattern of the past and had Scripture to back it up. The last three months of Hattie's life, she would faint if she tried to stand up. Once before she had passed out in the hospital when they asked her to stand so that they could check her blood pressure. That time, she made a remarkable recovery because the doctors increased the volume of her blood by a transfusion. During this longer siege, my mind was directed to the Scripture, "They that wait upon the Lord shall . . . walk and not faint."(Isa 40:31) When I told Hattie, she commented that she would work on the "not fainting" now and on the "walking" later. Sarah made friends at work. Everyone seemed to like her. The boss complimented her on her attitude.

A friend encouraged Jim and Susie by saying that their daughter didn't walk until she was eighteen months old. By the time of this comment, that girl was a normal, happy teenager. Everything was going to be all right! Jim and Susie came to believe that Arthur's delay in walking was some kind of a fluke. He seemed so normal otherwise. All of us had life figured out.

John had his hopes built up also. As the close-knit group approached Jerusalem for what proved to be the last time, there was anticipation that Jesus was about to spring the surprise and announce that He was the King of Israel. A pattern was established. His miracles could be read as signs that pointed to the imminent proclamation. John wanted to be on the inside track and so with his brother James, he approached Jesus about special places of power to be granted to them. The Scripture came to their minds that promised a kingdom of ever-increasing influence. (Isaiah 9:6)

With a cozy confidence, John approached the Passover meal with a sense of security. His life had meaning in the relationships that he had established with the men around the table. The love that he felt, satisfied him that all was well. In a few short hours, all that was to change. Into this tranquil situation, Jesus became "troubled in spirit and testified and said, 'Truly, truly I say unto you, one of you shall betray me.'"(John 13:21) The group was in a state of shock. "I can't believe that I heard Him correctly," and yet He used the "formula" that He had always used when He wanted us to pay strict attention to what He was saying. Peter gestured to John to find out more. John discovered that Jesus was referring to Judas, but he still couldn't grasp the thought.

He was still puzzling over this unthinkable thought when he became conscious that Jesus was speaking again. "Now is the Son of Man glorified and God is glorified in Him. If God is glorified in Him, God will glorify Him in Himself and shall straightway glorify Him. Little children, yet a little while I am with you. You will look for me and as I said to the Jews, 'Where I am going you cannot come,' now I am saying that to you also. A new commandment I give unto you: that you love one another as I have loved you. . . By this shall all men know that you are my disciples, if you love one another." (John 13:31-35). Some comfort in the expression of His love, but what is this He is saying? He is leaving? What was happening to the little scenario that John had allowed to form in his subconscious? Life's meaning was fading fast.

Now came another blow — Peter, the strong spokesman for the group raised the questions that were in everyone's mind, "Where are you going? Why can't we come along?" Peter further declared, "I am willing to die for You." The devastating reply: "Really, Peter? You may sincerely feel that way now, but before morning you will deny any acquaintance with Me at least three times." John's mind is reeling. He can't believe that all that he had lived for in the past three years was about to slip from his grasp.

He must have felt like I felt when I looked at the monitor that displayed Hattie's heartbeat and realized that she was dying, or like Sarah felt when the boss said, "Pack up your things and don't come back," or like Jim and Susie felt when they read the diagnosis. A real part of our lives was slipping away from us. Life's meaning was awash.

Our group pauses to consider what gives meaning to life. Jim suggests: "I believe that our relationships play a big part in giving meaning to life." Susie responds: "That helps me! I have been focusing on what we have lost — our son's health — instead of remembering that he is still alive and is still our son!" I reflect: "During our earliest days, mother becomes the tie to the external world and through her we begin to interpret life." Sarah contributes: "We are frequently judged by the relationships that we have developed. We are a Christian, wife, a mother, a Sunday School teacher, an ex-switchboard operator," she gives a little chuckle and then continues, "or some other combination of complex relationships. When some link in this chain of relationships that gives meaning to life is broken, reevaluation is necessary." We all remark: "And that is painful!" Jim muses: "How can we cope? What can hold us steady in the midst of shaking foundations?"

We resume our visit to the upper room in Jerusalem. John becomes aware that Jesus is still speaking. He is talking to the whole group now and not just to Peter. He is saying, "Don't be upset in your heart. Believe in God." Ah! here is some help. To believe in God assures him that there is some meaning in life. Events are not just random. There is some order in the things that happened and are about to happen. If John is patient and thinks about it, there will be answers to his questions or he will realize that his questions are nonsense. (Sometimes our questions are about as meaningless as: "Why is round not square?") We look at each other and remark: "Let's not lose our faith in God."

John continues to ponder: "To believe in God guarantees that the Ultimate Reality is good." The idea pops into my head: "With my limited view of life, sometimes what I think is good is really bad and vice versa." From the beginning of His ministry, Jesus had talked about being "lifted up," "glorified," and other expressions that told the disciples of His death. Coming down from the Mount of Transfiguration, Jesus became even more specific. They were to tell no one of what they had just seen until "The Son of Man is risen from the dead." He also said that Elijah had already come as promised and that he had been killed. "Likewise, the Son of Man will suffer at their hands." Peter took Him to task about saying such things. Jesus was just trying to protect them from developing false concepts about His mission and ministry. Now He is saying that His death was imminent, but John is thinking: "that can't be good." Jesus seems to read his thoughts and assures the disciples that it is a good thing for Him to leave them. "It is a good thing that I am going away, for if I don't go away the Comforter will not come."(John 16:7)

Jim also suggests that: "To believe in God gives us something that is permanent in our life." This is illustrated by John's remembering that the God that he knew was the God of the Scriptures (our Old Testament). He is depicted as the victorious Lord of Hosts, the Rock in the wilderness, a Refuge, the One in control. "The eternal God is our Refuge and supporting you are the everlasting arms." (Deuteronomy 33:27)

During Hattie's extended illness, one of my colleagues asked me: "How do you stand it?" I went into detail about my "special" promise that Hattie would walk and not faint. I concluded by saying that I did not know whether it would be on the streets of Florence, or on the streets of some heavenly city. Little did I know at the time that it would be the latter. To believe in God furnishes foundation for belief in the permanence of life.

Jesus continues: "Believe also in Me." This is another step away from the brink of meaninglessness. He is saying "Trust me. I am the Way, the Truth, and the Life." John had followed Him up to this point. He had trusted Jesus. Now it seemed that Jesus was letting him down by leaving him. Confusion reigns in John's mind. Jesus urges John to continue to trust Him. "I know what I am doing. The Father and I have agreed on this path and now I am just doing what He wants me to. Look at the works which I have done up until this time. These are signs that I am worthy of your trust. Now the next step is for me to leave this world through death. Believe me that this is not the end of everything. I have a mission on the other side of the picture and part of that mission is to prepare for your arrival at my Father's house."

I asked the group: "What does 'believing in Christ' mean to you?" Susie suggests: "To believe in Christ also tells us that love is eternal. Jesus ministry was full of teachings about love. If this life is all that there is, love is futile. It is simply an instrument of torture. Our love for Arthur is pure misery if we don't believe in Christ." I join in with this comment: "Hattie taught me to love. She was unselfish. She thought of others first. She would do things for me when it pushed her to the limit. One day she had been quite sick when I left for the university. I came home at noon to check up on her and found her propped up against the ironing board ironing my shirts. She wanted me to look nice! That is only one incident among so many. To suppose that all that she taught me about love is wasted would make it unbearable. To believe in Christ is to believe that, 'because I live, you will live also.' (John 14:19) Hattie's love for me and her family is still alive." Sarah wipes a tear and says softly: "My late husband loved Mike and me. I believe Christ is assuring me that if I believe in Him, though I should die, yet shall I live. He said 'Whosoever lives and believes in Me shall never die.' We shall be united again as a family."

I muse out loud: "To believe in Christ is to be assured that He is with us. He wanted us to know that 'if you love me you will keep my words and the Father will love you and we will come and live with you.' (John 14:23) Furthermore, we are told of a companionship that is closer than even human ties. Jesus promised to 'pray to the Father that another Counselor would come to abide with us forever. Even the Spirit of Truth whom the world cannot receive because it does not see Him nor know Him. But,' Jesus continues, 'He is now with you and shall be in you.' God Himself, in the person of the Holy Spirit, is available to us without respect to location."

"John, keep your perspective. You accepted my challenge about three years ago when I called you to be a fisher of men. Now I am giving you another challenge. It is imperative for Me and in your best interest for Me to go to my Father. Of course that means that I am leaving this world and ending this first phase of our relationship. It is the beginning of another phase that will last as long as you live. I am not asking you to avoid the tough places in life. I am not asking that you deny reality and escape through flights of fantasy. You will face all that this earthly life has to hit you with, but you will be the final winner. Believe in God, believe also in Me."

Across the years and miles, I believe that He is telling me today, "I came to you nearly fifty years ago with a challenge. You accepted the challenge. There have been times before when the road of life took some unexpected turns. Many of these, you have come to see, were in your best interest as when you left the pastoral ministry to teaching at the university. You have had many pleasant surprises; for example, when you trusted Me with your move to Tuscaloosa and you ended up with a Ph.D. I have helped you over rough places before as when your father died when you were only twenty years old. I know that Hattie's death is rough, but keep your perspective, believe in God, believe also in Me."

Sarah testifies: "He is telling me in my heart, 'I came to you forty one years ago and challenged you to trust Me with your life. I made you a minister's wife and mother. You have served Me faithfully.' Because of His message in my heart, I have a peace about the future. I am not sure what will happen, but I know that He will be with me."

Jim and Susie acknowledge that at this point, they feel

encouraged by our testimonies, but that their fall into the canyon has been too recent for them to speak with any conviction. Sarah and I assure them that it is all right and that God knows their heart. We all pray together.

We invite you to fill in your own story. Join us as we sit at the bottom of the canyon and reflect on these great truths. We are remodeling our worldview and invite you to examine yours. With this reconstructed view of things, we can begin to read some meaning back into our life. Yes, it is worth trying to get up and making it up the trail to the top of the mesa again. We believe in God and we also believe in Jesus Christ, His Son. Do you?

CHAPTER 4

FIGHTING DEPRESSION

Summary: *We meet Isabelle who has survived clinical depression with the aid of professional help. Now she joins us on the floor of the canyon. Non-clinical depression is a common experience. Many depressive feelings can be eased by discovering the cause of our depression, by seeking God's help in putting things in their proper perspective, and by discerning His plans for our future thus giving us hope.*

With the meaning of life beginning to return, I thought that there was hope that I might feel like a person again. Then this morning I woke up feeling as though a heavy stone were resting on my heart. I recognize the symptoms of depression. Depressive feelings come in many degrees — from the temporary quiet of a pensive mood to the deep-blue funk that may last for months. It is a common experience and I am sure that you have been there.

As a child I was taught in Sunday School that to be "down in the dumps" was a trick of the devil and such a depression could be remedied by singing loudly. As an adult, I discovered that exercising positive thinking does not always dispel the cloud or relieve the pressure of depression. From my study of the Bible, I decided that it is not sinful to be depressed — even clinical depression.

I met Isabelle at the bottom of the canyon. Isabelle became a Christian as a child. She maintained her faith through high school and college. After she earned an undergraduate degree she accepted a good job in an office with a Christian environment. While working there she continued her education and was awarded a Master of Science degree in Sociology. Her life seemed in order. One problem bothered her – she was still single. Then her mother died.

During the grieving process, Isabelle began to review her life's goals. As we mentioned in the previous chapter, life's meaning fades when trauma occurs. This calls for a reevaluation of our goals, priorities and values. Through this evaluation Isabelle maintained her Christian worldview. This established a foundation for further evaluation. She decided that she could be more effective in service to others if she had a doctor's degree in psychology. She explored the possibilities.

First step is to select a graduate school with a notable reputation in her selected field. She chose a prestigious university and applied. She received a letter of acceptance. This meant that she must quit her job and move to another city.

The next step was to select an advisor who would direct her program. The advisor in a Ph.D.(1 See endnote) program is extremely important. It is your advisor that helps you select what courses to take so that you can pass the exams. He knows who is doing original research in your selected field so that you won't have someone publish before you and thus derail your program. He helps steer your dissertation proposal through the committee. He makes suggestions as you do your original research. He reads the first draft of your dissertation and makes suggestions to change some of your vocabulary to include the latest "buzz words" in the field. He is your champion when you come to the oral defense of your dissertation. Sometimes, he helps you to get "published." He needs to be your friend. Isabelle was able to persuade a respected member of the faculty to be her advisor.

Things went well the first year. However, she was lonely. She was still single and her advisor, although married, let her know that he was available. She missed the wisdom of her mother's advice. She was also troubled with financial problems. Overall, though, she felt that she had made the right decision.

Her trouble in graduate school began the next year when she had a philosophical disagreement with one of the professors, we will call Dr. X. As a matter of principle, Isabelle felt obligated to discuss this with her professor. The professor misinterpreted Isabelle's motive and took offense at her apparent audacity. Isabelle dropped the class. After this conflict, Isabelle's advisor became ill and was no longer able to direct her research. Meanwhile, Dr. X became department head. Isabelle requested a new advisor. Dr. X ignored her request. She appealed to the Dean of the Graduate School who appointed Dr. X as her advisor. Stress is building. Her plans for a doctor's degree are in jeopardy.

When Isabelle completed all the requirements for her Ph.D. except writing and defending her dissertation, she decided to try to find employment in her field. She applied to states in different regions of the country that appealed to her. After several on site job interviews, she received a telephone interview from a distant state. After sifting all the data and considering the options, she decided to take the job offer in the distant state. Isabelle packed up and moved to the new location. She was hired by the State to work with troubled youth. During the telephone interview the environment was depicted as harmonious, the other professionals as cooperative, the administrators as supportive of innovation, and the youth as mildly troubled and therefore could be helped. The first day on the job was an eye-opener. The environment was shabby, the professionals backbiting, the administrators dictatorial and the troubled youth were mainly psychotic.

Isabelle was determined to make the best of a bad situation. She selected a few youth that showed some promise of salvaging. She developed a program for them and had them persuaded to cooperate. The prospect of implementing the program gave the young people hope. When the plan came before the administration, they sabotaged it. It wasn't long until they insist that Isabelle do several things that were unethical. Isabelle refused. They threatened to fire her but she wouldn't back down. Finally the administrators relented.

The extreme stress over a period of several years – mother's death, remaining single, two long moves, going to graduate school, losing her advisor to illness, controversy with current advisor, being lied to about her new job and the realization that all her plans were being frustrated – caused chemical changes in her body. She became suicidal. Not only had she fallen into the canyon, but into a pit at the bottom of the canyon. She needed professional help the get her chemistry back to normal. She needed a professional counselor to help her sort through the causes of her stress and get some relief. She needed to regain her perspective.

She went to a doctor who prescribed some anti-depressive medication. She found a Christian counselor who helped her sort her problems and suggested options to alleviate some of the stress. She was able to correct her worldview that had been distorted by stress. Having received help in her struggle against clinical depression, she now she joins us on the canyon floor as we all make our journey through depression – the blue funk that is governing our moods.

Our traumatic experiences have caused us to be depressed. We must recognize that this is not sinful. God is still in our lives. Join us on our journey through this difficulty. Perhaps by studying an incident in the life of Elijah, we can resolve some of the mystery of depression.

The depth of Elijah's depression is indicated by his prayer: "It is enough now, O Lord, take away my life; for I am not better than my fathers."(I Kings 19:4) Elijah was still a man of God, but was clearly depressed. The first step in fighting depression is to recognize its origin.

The causes of our depression are readily discernible: My wife of over thirty-five years had died. Sarah had lost her job without notice. Jim and Susie faced a bleak future for their son. Isabelle was recovering from clinical depression.

Looking at the story of Elijah more closely, we can recognize the origin of his depression. Part of his depression was biogenic. Clearly he was tired and hungry. He had just completed a grueling time in contest with the prophets of Baal, had prayed fervently for rain, and had run several miles, had rested only shortly and then proceeded on for many more miles until he felt it safe to stop for rest in a wilderness area. In his haste, he had not eaten properly.

Elijah's depression was also psychogenic. Imagine yourself in his position. For three years he had hidden from King Ahab. Then he felt that the Lord wanted him to have a show-down with the prophets of Baal. In his challenge to the people of Israel he had put it bluntly: ". . . and the God that answers by fire, let him be God."(I Kings 18:24) Since the group that had gathered agreed that it was a fair contest, Elijah felt that he would soon be a national hero and that the "God of Israel" would once again reign supreme in Israel. God dramatically answered Elijah's prayer for fire and the people seemed to unite behind him. It looked as though the people of Israel were ready to return to God. Elijah's popular support was obvious when the people helped him dispose of the prophets of Baal. Then when his prayer for rain was answered after three years of drought, it was reasonable to assume that there should be no doubt as to who was God. Elijah must have been on an all-time emotional high.

Then Queen Jezebel heard about the contest and Elijah's success and instead of acknowledging God and accepting His prophet, she put a price on his head. A friend carried the news to Elijah. He must have wondered, "Why does God allow that woman to live? She has swayed the public opinion to treat me as a villain instead of a champion!" Coming off an emotional high and being threatened with execution was reason enough for Elijah to be depressed.

One of the psychological needs of each of us is to be

accepted, to belong, to be loved. This need was not being met in Elijah's life at this time. He felt rejected, alone, and hated. Even though he had scored such a magnificent victory in the name of the Lord, he felt that he had failed. His mission was to turn Israel from her wicked ways. Mission was not accomplished.

Isabelle is recovering from her clinical depression but is still fighting a deep-blue funk. She went to church in search of people her age that might share her interests. One man warmed up to her and after a couple of meetings, she clearly recognized that he was psychotic and that she needed to flee this friendship before it became dangerous. A person at work is friendly but she does not share Isabelle's fundamental values. She is a "pain" because she ridicules Isabelle for her Christian perspective. Another Christian friend succumbed to the pressure of her "boy friend" and encourages Isabelle to find a man — any man — as the solution to her pain. Isabelle is beginning to feel isolated from everyone for her allegiance to God.

It doesn't take a doctor to tell me the source of my depression. Less than a year ago my wife died after a thirteen-year struggle with cancer. Our relationship had been ideal. We had never raised our voice at one another in more than thirty-five years of married life. If either of us felt anger or hurt arising over something the other had done, we would stop the discussion immediately. Hours later, or even the next day, we would discuss the incident. But we would always talk about it. We would not let it poison our marriage nor would we let discussing it in the heat of emotion allow us to say something that we would later regret. Hattie taught me many things. Now that she is gone, I miss her warm, caring attitude and her wise counsel. This leads to periods of depression like this one and feeling that God has forsaken me.

Elijah decided to fight depression by action. The angel of the Lord touched him and said, "Arise and eat." The angel had prepared the food but would not feed him. He needed to do some things for himself. Here is some advice that was given to me: "It is good to have friends to listen to you and offer to help you, but your depression will only deepen if you allow them to do everything for you." After a second meal, Elijah was ready to travel. His depression did not vanish immediately, but he had devised a plan of action and wisely started to follow through on it. He would go back to Horeb where Moses had talked with God.

In returning to Horeb, Elijah must have thought that he was returning to the origin of the revelation of God to Israel as a nation. Moses had climbed the mountain. The smoke, fire, earthquake had been among the physical manifestations of the power of God. Perhaps Elijah relived the scene in his imagination and hoped that by returning to the physical location of the original revelation, he would find the secret of his failure and Moses' success. God had answered Elijah by fire and rain. Israel had rejected this evidence. Moses had brought the Children of Israel to the base of the mountain. After three days of preparation and anticipation, they were ready to be introduced to their God. The top of the mountain disappeared in smoke, fire danced among the rocks, the whole mountain shook as though it were about to be destroyed. The "sound of the trumpet" was so loud that it hurt. The people were afraid that they were about to perish. But it was on this mountain that Moses had talked with God. Elijah had apparently forgotten the fickleness of the people that Moses dealt with and how many times they had "angered" God, for example, the Golden Calf incident while Moses was still on the mountain. (Exodus 32).

Elijah hiked across the wilderness, finally found the mountain, climbed the mountain, discovered the "cleft in the rock" where Moses had hidden to protect himself from death at a complete vision of God. Elijah crawled into the cave. He curled up in a corner. He waited. He pondered the question, "What am I doing here? — I am tired of fighting the crowd. I don't need the fickle crowd anyway. Even God doesn't seem interested any more. O, why was I born?" His depression developed into a large dose of self-pity, which was short-circuiting his vision. He could see only himself and his plight. He griped, "I have been very jealous for the Lord God of Hosts: for the children of Israel have forsaken Thy covenant, thrown down Thine altars, and slain Thy prophets with the sword; and I, even I only, am left; and they seek my life, to take it away." (I Kings 19:10) He couldn't remember Obadiah, who "greatly feared the Lord" (I Kings 18:3), or any of the other faithful followers of God. His self-pity was pushing him toward the edge of despair. Instead of taking the opportunity to developing an objective view of his life and accomplishments, he was choosing only to look at his failure to win Israel.

The consensus here is that when we are depressed, we can see only our failures, losses, inadequacies, and frustrations. That is why it is important for us to regain our perspectives.

He is told to stand in the mouth of the cave. Then there is a display of great physical power, just like the "Good Old Days". Wind and earthquake throwing rocks around. Fire dancing from ledge to ledge. Elijah's adrenaline starts pumping. "It is worth the trip! But wait! God isn't in the display." God will not be limited to a small repertoire of action. Elijah needs to realize that even though God had answered by fire and the prophets of Baal had been slain, the true issues that Elijah was to address were moral in nature and not predominantly physical. Finally, Elijah's special revelation of God comes in a most surprising manner for this boisterous prophet: "a still, small voice". Gently, quietly, but firmly, God speaks to His faithful servant.

Recalling a journey into my past is helping me regain my perspective. For me regaining my perspective and the realizing that God has not forsaken me is proving to be the best relief for depression. I recall that four months after my wife's death, I visited Vermont where my four children were born. I worshipped in the church that Hattie and I had served as pastors for seven years. The response of our many friends was heart-warming. The community had changed. The people had grown older, but the warmth of their reception was unquestionable. Is God helping me to realize that those years that Hattie and I spent ministering to people were well spent? We had not lived in vain. We still live in the lives of those people.

I recall visiting Niagara Falls. In the more than twenty years since Hattie and I had visited the falls, there had been considerable erosion. The American Falls especially had changed and as I remember the trip I am forced to realize that even things as enduring as this natural wonder are subject to change with the years.

I recall visiting the graves of my mother and father, and am reminded of how Hattie, though weakened by disease, stood by my side when my mother died. She insisted on making the trip of approximately 3000 miles to help me bury her. The memory of her courage lives on as part of me.

I recall visiting the scenes of our first pastorate. I remember how we nearly starved to death. Many Christians of other denominations brought us food and coal. There were times when it looked as though God didn't care or had forgotten where He had left us. Just as our health was about to be permanently damaged by malnutrition, God sent in a call to another church. God had not deserted us after all.

I recall visiting Kentucky, where God led me out of the pastorate into a wider ministry. Before I moved there to accept a teaching position in the high school, I understood that the district superintendent had a church waiting for me. When I arrived, he had placed someone else in that position. Hattie was never happy in Kentucky, but she didn't complain. If that was where God wanted us, that was where we wanted to be. The local church that we attended was incredibly poor. At one time someone said to me "Cheer up, things could be worse!" So I did and they got. But when things were about to become intolerable, God opened a place for me in the university. Once again, I had to acknowledge that God had not abandoned me.

I recall my son and daughter traveling with me on my journey. Don insisted on driving when the weather was bad and the driving difficult. Julia found many ways to express her delight that we were together. Their love, kindness, and consideration seep into my consciousness with the message that I am indeed a fortunate man to have so much left.

On arriving home, I thought of one time when I had brought Hattie home from the hospital. I was helping her into the house, essentially carrying her, and she exclaimed, "Honey, my feet won't do what I tell them to." She was never able to walk again. I read "The Lord God is my strength, and he will make my feet like hinds' feet, and he will make me to walk upon mine high places." (Habakkuk 3:19) I was encouraged to think that God would perform a miracle and she would be walking around again in the high-heeled shoes that she loved. When she died, I felt that God had forgotten His promises. Journeying back into our past helps me to remember that God does not always do things like we expect Him to, but He does work in our lives. With this renewed perspective, my depression is not so deep now. I think of Hattie walking on her high places in heaven. It helps to remember that trip.

God gave Isabelle a dream the other night. She dreamed of being chased by a group of people, many of whom she recognized as being the ones that are causing her pain. They were gaining on her. She came to the top of a long staircase and started down. Near the top, she tripped and tumbled rapidly down the whole length of the stairs. At the bottom, she looked up and the crowd was gone. She was in a realm of soft, warm light. As her eyes began to focus, she saw some of her friends from days gone by. Then she saw her mother coming toward her. Her mother picked her up so gentle. The pain was gone. Once again she felt loved and accepted. Then she awoke. This experience is helping Isabelle to cope. It is like visiting the future that contains the past.

You say: "It is impossible for me to leave my present circumstances and journey back into the past and God has not favored me with a comforting dream." Do lack of finances, current employment, obligations of various sorts keep you from making the physical journey as Elijah and I did? Don't give up! If you have a photo album or diary, you can make the journey in your imagination. If you have nothing of that sort, take time to jot down in a few words some reminders of your personal history: your first job, your wedding, the first birthday that you became aware that "life was passing you by" (for me it was my twenty-fifth birthday), some significant successes, some significant failures, some significant losses, some decisions that changed the course of your life, or any other things which will help you to review your life. Then prayerfully consider your past asking God to use this to help you regain your perspective.

I must carefully reject the temptation to live in the past. I am aware that the past is a great place to visit if it will help me to recover my perspective, but I must also realize that there is a future for me. Isabelle gains comfort from the dream, but is still aware that she is living in the real world. She realizes that there is a future and therein there is hope. This seemed to come as a surprise to Elijah when God talked with him on the mountain. The first word that God said in response to Elijah's complaint was: "Go!" Now God is prescribing the action. "Elijah, you have work to do." God's charge to him even sent him to a foreign country to enlist an alien in the work of God: ". . . anoint Hazael to be king over Syria."(I Kings 19:15) Jezebel and Ahab are not immortal: ". . . and Jehu the son of Nimshi shalt thou anoint to be king over Israel."(I Kings 19:16) He seemed to instruct Elijah: "Your dramatic work of fire from heaven and rain after three years of severe drought are not the only work I have for you to do. You are to work for me behind the scenes also." To help meet the need for companionship, God selected Elisha to be Elijah's apprentice.

All this before God answered the bitter complaint of Elijah. In the depths of his gloom, the prophet had thought that He alone was lifting up the banner of righteousness. He alone was fighting the forces of idolatry and other evil. He alone was serving the true God. Now God answers his anguished cry, "Yet I have left me seven thousand in Israel, all the knees which have not bowed unto Baal, and every mouth which has not kissed him." (I Kings 19:18) God seemed to want Elijah to understand that He works through people. God's resources were not as limited as some would expect. The stormy prophet was one of the people used by God, but not the only one. Furthermore, Elijah was treading very close to the dangerous ground of self-righteous pride.

I must face up to the fact that my work is not yet done. Even though a significant part of me died when Hattie died, I still have some very real obligations. I have thought about how much harder it would have been on my children if I had died with Hattie. I have an obligation to my children. They still need the warmth and love of a parent and now I am obliged to do double duty. I am still Professor of Physics at the university. The students have helped me to feel needed and accepted. My faculty and staff are very support- ive. They insist that they need me as Head of the Department to run the department. I am encouraged to pursue my research.

Friends have asked me to write this book and let them have copies so that they can profit from my experience. I do not feel that my experience is unique. There are many that suffer even more severe trials than I, but God has placed me in unusual circumstances. As a minister without obligation to a particular congregation, I have the freedom to explore my emotions and faith without fear of offending anyone under my charge. With my Ph.D. in physics and my seminary degree in biblical literature, I am uniquely equipped to minister in many ways. This is my present vision. I may realize only part of these dreams. As long as I live, I plan to do my best to fulfill God's plan for my life. It helps my attitude to think that God can use me. The pressure has let up some since I have applied the lessons that I have learned in this study. My depression has lightens.

Isabelle is reminded that she has a dissertation to write and defend. She has learned that even when life seems to be at a dead end, God has plans for her future. She has started to a different church and finds that there are other young people that share her values. A "small group" in the church is proving to be a support for her. She is looking for another job where she can use her skills to make a difference in the lives of some young people. She is not completely out of the woods, but, like the rest of us, is making great progress toward a productive life.

CHAPTER 5

FACING STRESS AND FAILURE

Summary: Sometimes stress is so severe that we can't function properly. Stress can also cause us to neglect our highest priorities. Problems that frustrate our sense of success escalate our stress. Larry is a case in point. Brooding over the problems only makes it worse. We should try to analyze each problem to see it there is anything that we can do to correct the situation. In addition, hopefully, we can find a support group. If we look diligently, we can probably find some positive aspect of the situation and maximize its benefit.

Meet Larry. Larry is an enterprising young man. He married his high school sweetheart, Cynthia. Larry is a man with class. He is always neat in his appearance. He puts a person at ease when you are with him. He is a salesman with a heart. He took a job selling life insurance because he wanted people to have the resources necessary to meet their needs in a time of crisis. He and his wife were active in church, being a model couple for young people. They have many friends.

Larry thought that he could be a more effective salesman if he had some additional education. Cynthia urged him to do it. He and Cynthia moved to a nearby city so that Larry could attend the university. Larry enrolled in the university, majoring in marketing and with a minor in management. Cynthia got a good-paying, non-challenging job. Because of their personalities, they soon made friends. From all appearances they were still the model couple. Larry's school work went well but at the expense of the time that he could share with his wife. The couple spent little time together in their comfortable apartment. Cynthia became bored with her job. She missed her old friends from the big city.

Although they now lived in a small town, there were symphonies, a variety of musical artist's concerts, dramatic productions and social activities. But who wants to attend these alone? So she would sit alone in the apartment idly flipping through the TV channels, nibbling on junk food and showing signs of depression while Larry spent his time at the university whether in the library or in study groups. Even the church didn't seem to bring relief from the boredom that imprisoned Cynthia. She even started to attend a different church from Larry, each one going alone. She tried alcohol. But drinking at home alone didn't deaden the pain. They were gradually growing apart — Larry moving on with his life while Cynthia's life seemed to be on hold. The light at the end of the tunnel was that in a few months Larry would graduate and then they could move on with their lives — hopefully together.

When he graduated, he hoped to get a job with a prosthesis company. However, he was immediately hired by an engineering firm to sell an industrial product. The future looked promising. His marketing skills were superb. However, the job required mechanical engineering skills that he did not have. Furthermore, he had to travel over a tri-state area that meant that he was frequently away from home. Cynthia was waiting for the "pot of gold at the end of the rainbow." Larry and his wife were disappointed with his job. Larry quit and they moved back to a large city. Larry found a steady job in retail sales. Cynthia was not satisfied. She thought that, with Larry's education and the sacrifices that she had made, he should have a job with a "high sounding title in a prestigious company" making enough money to support the life style that she fantasized. She hoped that they could spend more time together. She blamed Larry for not reading her thoughts. One night she told him that she wanted out. For her, the light at the end of the tunnel had gone out. He was dumbfounded.

After considerable persuasion on his part, she agreed to stay for a six-month trial period to resolve the insecurity problems that Cynthia claimed that she felt. Larry applied himself diligently to his work. He came home from work as soon as he could and catered to Cynthia's whims. She remained cool. It seems that their interests had changed. At the end of six months, Larry's family fell apart. "Why?"

Larry is trying to fit the pieces back together. The haunting question in Larry's mind is: "How did I fail? What did I do wrong? Cynthia and I have worked in the church giving it top priority. This should have been a good foundation for our marriage. The church provided meaning for our lives. The first hint I had that something might be wrong was that Cynthia started drinking and attending another church. I thought she understood that I was working hard to provide for her. Probably I should not have taken that high-paying job that required so much travel. I did well except when I needed engineering skills. After that, I thought the move to the big city with more opportunities to become involved in a larger church and make new friends would help. Is her loneliness because we have grown apart — our common interests diminished? Is it because she feels insecure because or our recent moves and lifestyle changes? I have failed miserably! But why. . . ? It was twenty years and I thought that our marriage was working, that it was forever. How could I have been so blind?"

Larry's stress of trying to improve himself so that he could better serve others pushed him to neglect that one person that really counted in his life. Late night study sessions held his attention. She felt neglected but she kept telling herself: "It's only for a short time." Perhaps she should have taken some classes at the university to enrich her life. Later, his job that required him to be away from home further eroded his relationship with his wife. His priorities became confused. His idea of "what's best for you, Cynthia," didn't match her idea.

Sarah is dealing with a sense of failure also. Prior to her husband's death, she had been a full-time homemaker and mother except for six months when she was a "short-order" cook in order to help the family out of a financial bind. It was amazing that she was hired so quickly after her husband's death. But now she had been fired. She had failed because she was not given any "on the job training." This did not ease the pain of failure.

Even though we are at the bottom of a spiritual canyon, we all must function in the real world. My marriage is over. My wife is dead. Much of my stress is related to success or failure in my work. I am feeling the pressure from my social environment to succeed. I live in a success-oriented society. The problem is that, for the most part, society thinks of success in terms of prestige, power, popularity, and economic status. For me, these criteria are not applicable and Sarah would be satisfied with a job – any honest job.

While we are in the canyon, perhaps what we need is to look for a new concept of "success". It seems to me that success should be judged by each individual with respect to his purpose. Success is related to goals. Larry was a success in meeting his goals of getting more education and acquiring a high-paying job but a failure with respect to his marriage. Our missions in life must be defined before our accomplishments can be judged as success or failure. Even then, there is the problem what percentage of attempted projects must be completed successfully before one can be pronounced a success? Or conversely, how many times must we fail before we should consider ourselves failures?

I have met some people who are functionally successful, but consider themselves failures because of some nagging problem in their life. Perhaps one time in their life they made a bad choice and since then they have been berating themselves as a failure. I suppose that I could have developed that complex over an incident that made me feel embarrassed and stupid. I was playing baseball one afternoon while I was in college. I had made a clean hit into right field. The fielder threw the ball to the first baseman, but I was there in plenty of time. No problem! I thought the first baseman had thrown the ball to the pitcher. The pitcher turned to face the batter and get his signal from the catcher. I stepped off the base to take a little lead and the first baseman tagged me out. I had become the victim of their charade. I felt stupid! But in reality, I did not feel as though I failed because I have no ambitions to become a professional baseball player. It was only a "scrub" game and I was really just representing me. Under other circumstances, I might have judged myself to have failed if the same thing happened.

Stress is hindering my ability to make good decisions. At times, I have not done as well in grasping an opportunity as I should. As a result, I fail! When this happens, I am learning not to judge myself as a failure, but face the problem in the whole context of my life. Paul provides us with a pattern in the one of his letters.

When Paul had his vision of Christ on the road to Damascus, he was given a mission. He was to preach, evangelize, and establish churches. He found many opportunities to preach and evangelize. He established churches in many cities that were fundamentally pagan. It looks to me as though he was a success. But he talks of a time when he failed: "When I came to Troas to preach Christ's gospel, and a door was opened unto me of the Lord, I had no rest in my spirit, because I did not find Titus my brother: but taking my leave of them, I went from thence to Macedonia." (2 Corinthians 2:12,13) This is an amazing thing. He recognized an opportunity. He sensed that it was "of the Lord", but he failed to take advantage of it. What could have stressed him out so much and how did he handle it?

His action tells us that he did not to brood over the problem. He only casually mentions it here because he is telling the Corinthians of his concern for them. He could have thought:

"If only I had trusted God more . . ."

"If only I had concentrated on the present circumstances . . ."
"If only I had exercised more self-discipline . . ."
"If only I had prayed more earnestly about the situation . . ."
"If only I had not worried . . ."

He obviously didn't. He did not deny that he was upset. He did not try to hide his feelings under a cloak of hypocrisy. Even when he reached Macedonia he confesses "our flesh had no rest, but we were troubled on every side; without were fightings, within were fears."(2 Corinthians 7:5) On the other hand, he did not flagellate himself about the lost opportunity.

Because of the stress he was experiencing, he had temporarily lost his power to concentrate on the thing that he loved to do so much. Yet he was able to recognize the source of his stress. The problem was the situation at Corinth. Paul had preached at Corinth and established a church there. It was a city that was noted for its licentious living. With little moral training or background, the church had some difficulty in developing a clear concept of Christian ethics and morality. In addition to that, there was considerable dispute over the superiority of one clique over another. The church was about to destroy itself. To compound the problem, it appeared that there were some men who arrived at Corinth claiming to be true missionaries, denigrated Paul's ministry and cast doubts on his authority. Apparently there was someone in the Corinthian church who was only too willing to jump on the "denounce Paul" bandwagon. This problem consumed Paul's thoughts. It controlled his emotions. It sapped his energy. He couldn't function properly.

However, Paul was fortunate. He had friends and coworkers who helped him in the task of spreading the gospel. Timothy was like a son to him. Luke was his physician and friend. Silas was his close associate. Titus was a trusted colleague. There were others that Paul could depend on for support. In this case, Titus was selected to carry out a special mission.

As Head of the Department of Physics, I am responsible for schedules, budgets, appointments, and decisions that represent

the department in the total university program. I take my responsibilities seriously. This last semester, I was not performing at a
level that met my standard. I was late with some of my schedules.
I forgot some of my appointments. In other situations, I could not
think clearly. Stress sometimes made me sleepy as a means to
escape reality and give relief from the pressure. In one meeting of
the department heads I dozed off and started to snore. My
colleagues' laughs woke me! I laughed with them. I know the
source of my stress is the death of my wife, Hattie. Fortunately, I
have a wonderful team surrounding me. When I said in a department meeting that if I didn't get on top of the problem I would
resign, they expressed support for my leadership. That afternoon
they presented me with a document:

YE OLDE VOTE OF CONFIDENCE
We appreciate your efforts on behalf of the department
and believe that you are doing an excellent job as our "Boss".
Please do <u>not</u> think of bailing out.
SINCERELY

It was signed by all seven of the members of the department.
I am fortunate, as was Paul, to have such a fine support team that
is always willing to step in and take up the slack when any one of
the other members of the team is having problems.

Larry found help in the church. He sought and found
forgiveness. He joined a Sunday School class (a "small group")
made up of people with similar interests. His colleagues at work
provide some camaraderie to buoy up his spirits. This relieves
some of the stress.

You object that you do not have the support that you feel you
need. One of my daughters works in a college also. When her
mother died, she experienced stress as I did. She did have my
support and the support of her brother and sisters but we lived at
some distance from her. When she returned to work after the
funeral, she was expected to perform as though nothing happened.

A colleague of hers, who had lost her husband three years before, should have been understanding. Instead, she said to my daughter, "You don't have a problem! You only lost your mother but I lost MY husband." No help there! My daughter found help through prayer addressed to a loving heavenly Father, through reading the Bible and devotional material and by visualizing the "everlasting arms" (Deuteronomy 33:27).supporting her while she received comfort from the Holy Spirit Who was sent by the "Man of sorrows" Who was Himself acquainted with grief. (Isaiah 53:3).

Other aspects of Paul's experience would point the way to help even without the team. By example he would tell us to do what we can about the stressful situation. Often this requires seeking more information. When you understand the situation more fully, you can take intelligent action or calm your troubled mind. Paul seems to have sent Timothy to Corinth to help the church. (1 Corinthians 16:10-11) It might appear that the rebellious faction did not "conduct him forth in peace". Paul became aware of more trouble in the church so he made a quick trip to straighten it out. (2 Corinthians 10:1) Ugly scenes followed. The upshot of this action led to his leaving without resolving the conflict. In a sharply worded letter, he promised to return soon and settle the matter. (2Corinthains10:8-11) Instead, he sent Titus as his trouble-shooter. Titus was to gather information about the situation and report back to Paul. They were to meet either in Troas or Macedonia. Paul was anxious to receive information about the results of his action. When the news came it was good news. "Nevertheless God, that comforts those that are cast down, comforted us by the coming of Titus. And not by his coming only but by the consolation wherewith he was comforted in you." (2 Corinthians 7:6-7) Then he confessed that he had experienced some misgivings about the stern letter that he had sent: "For though I made you sorry with a letter, I do not repent, though I did repent. . . . Now I rejoice, not that you were made sorry, but that you sorrowed to repentance." (2 Corinthians 7:8-9)

Is there some information that can help us devise a plan of

action? We prayed for guidance. We are discovering that the kind of action depends upon the cause of the stress. Many have written books or magazine articles about how they handled problems similar to ours. Becoming unemployed, going through a divorce, experiencing the death of a family member, trusting someone and having them turn on you, being misunderstood, having your reputation ruined by someone's lies, being chronically ill, or any number of incidents have been written about by other people. Sometimes the best action is to learn how others handled their situation and then adapt their methods to your situation.

Of course the Bible is a great resource book on handling stress. Observe Joseph being lied about and put in prison as a result. (Genesis 39) Jesus was betrayed by one of his close associates. (John 13:21ff) It also gives advice about forgiving those who have "wronged" you. If you have been at fault, admit it and ask forgiveness. Tough action, but it clears the cobwebs out of your soul.

What action did I take to reduce my stress? I sought more information. In addition to reading a number of books, I obtained a copy of the autopsy performed on my late wife. From the study of this report, I was able to draw some helpful conclusions. The immediate cause of death was a virulent strain of pneumonia. I knew this at the time of her death. I had speculated about her probable physical condition if she had lived. From the autopsy I discovered that, had she survived her pneumonia, she would probably required a respirator to maintain her life. She would have been bedfast, had little control over her body functions and would have experience periods of extreme weakness. There was extensive damage to her brain stem. It appears that the treatment that had prolonged her life for thirteen years by destroying her cancer was what finally destroyed her ability to fight off death. This information helped me realize that the decisions that Hattie and I had made along the way in her fight for survival were probably good ones. Also, her death was more merciful than her continued existence as an invalid. She had always been an active woman and it hurt both of us to experience her paralysis. She fought her disability with dignity and courage, without complaining, but she did not want to be a burden to anyone. The information in the autopsy helped me to become reconciled to her death.

Larry is talking with others who are grieving. He is discovering how others have adjusted to life after a divorce. He has talked with the pastoral staff at his church to learn biblical principles that are guiding his actions toward healing. Sarah is searching the papers and asking friends, looking for a job. This time, she will insist on some "on the job training" and a detailed job description to learn what is expected of her.

Paul's mental health in this situation is seen by the fact that he was able to look at the positive side of the experience. Instead of constantly thinking about the opportunity lost by his upsetting stress, he looked at the whole experience as an overall success. He exclaims: "Now thanks be unto God, which always causes us to triumph in Christ, and makes manifest the savour of his knowledge by us in every place. For we are unto God a sweet savour of Christ, in them that are saved, and in them that perish: To the one we are the savour of death unto death; and to the other the savour of life unto life. And who is sufficient for these things?" (2 Corinthians 2:14-16)

In the Corinthian situation, Paul had clearly worried about the outcome. He had wondered if he had handled the situation properly. He was so stressed that he passed up an opportunity to evangelize. In spite of all these negative things, when he looked back on the situation, he thanked God, Who makes us to be more than conquerors. I probably would have bemoaned the lost opportunity. Paul looks at this as a victory. Instead of being lost in the details of his life, he was continually reminded of the total picture. He was so amazed by the grace of God that he considered himself a slave to Christ. Being a captive of Christ and being "displayed" in a His triumphal march was, to Paul, a distinct privilege. He was exultant when Christ, his Leader, was successful. This attitude toward his surrender to Christ was as an invigorating breath of fresh air to some, while to others it was a poison gas.

His humility and sincerity made him "sufficient unto these things." (2 Corinthians 2:16-17)

We are reminding ourselves that God has forgiven us as Christians. To get past this sense of failure, we must forgive ourselves. Some of us are finding this tough. In theory, if we focus on what God has done and is doing <u>for</u> us, we will not be dangerously proud of what God is doing <u>through</u> us. If we stay completely surrendered to God, He will help us to develop proper attitudes and a clear perspective. We are finding that it is working.

Larry is trying to forgive himself and move on with his life. He is convinced that God can use this experience to help him grow spiritually. He feels that someway God may be able to use this experience, difficult as it is, to put him in a position to help someone else. His situation is more difficult than mine because Cynthia is still alive. He has a problem with closure.

How does this relate to my situation? I confess that for a long time after Hattie's death I had considerable difficulty in thanking God. In our local church on Wednesday evening during the service we have a "thanksgiving" prayer by someone whom the pastor selects. When I felt the least thankful, he would invariably call on me to pray! Hattie's death had left me angry. It was a generalized anger. It was not focused on anything or any one. I wasn't consciously angry with God, or Hattie, or the doctors and hospital staff. I was simply in an angry mood.

I wondered about Hattie's present state. I read all the right passages in the Bible, but most of them seemed to refer to the state of the dead after the final resurrection. I read books about the intermediate state. I read several books about near-death experiences. It seemed that knowledge of the intermediate state was accessible only by faith. I finally realized that faith is based on a decision. I considered the alternatives that were available to me regarding her present state. Annihilation, soul-sleep, purgatory, and paradise were all considered. Upon deciding to investigate evidence for a conscious state in the presence of Christ, I found some Scripture that seemed to form a foundation for faith in this hypothesis. Jesus said to the repentant thief on the cross, "Verily I say unto you, today you will be with me in paradise." (Luke 23:43) This was prior to the resurrection and implies consciousness of being in the presence of Christ. In relating his "near-death" experience, Paul says that he was "caught up into paradise and heard unspeakable words." (2 Corinthians 12:4) Also Paul writes that he hopes the second advent will occur before he experiences death but he is reconciled to death if it should come first because "to be absent from the body is to be present with the Lord." (2 Corinthians 5:1-8)

My Sunday School class has helped me to filter my thoughts and I can now thank God. I thank God that Hattie, who suffered pain and physical degeneration, is now in the presence of her beloved Redeemer and exploring the vistas of paradise. Hattie wanted my support in her struggle against disease. On one occasion when she was in intense pain she mentioned death and I said that I would not be selfish and ask her to remain in her present condition. Later, when she felt some better, she said that I had said the wrong thing. She had wanted my assurance that I needed her. I really did! After that we did not talk much about death. However, on two occasions we talked specifically about the possibility of her death. There is an old song that suggests that we will wait for our loved ones "just inside the eastern gate". I told her not to wait for me there in the crowd, but to explore heaven and when I arrive she can show me things that she has discovered. I can now thank God in the confidence that Hattie is not suffering, is conscious, and enjoying the "presence" of her Christ. I rejoice in the hope that we will be together again and will be able to share the experiences each of us has had in the interim. I have much to thank God for.

Are you having problems due to stress? Are you troubled with a sense of failure? Jim and Susie are very stressed. However, they are not feeling so much a sense of failure as a sense of helpless. They are faced with a number of decisions that will affect their lives and the lives of their boys. How to handle Arthur's frustration at school? Should they "home school" him? How to treat Arthur as part of the family? Should they discipline him and help him develop psychologically or let him have free reign and develop the attitude of a victim? (This may seem to be a "duh" unless you have had to face it. You love your child and want to protect him. You want to make up to him for all the things of which he has been deprived. Your heart tells you that he suffers enough from disease and should therefore have everything that he wants. Your mind tells you that he needs to be treated much like any six-year-old.) What about Ken? How can they find enough time to keep him from feeling left out? He must also be afraid that he will develop the same problem as Arthur. How should Jim and Susie reassure him?

To cope with these and other problems, Jim and Susie are gathering as much information as possible. They are connecting with a "help group" of other parents that have similar problems. Their friends at church are helping by praying and encouraging them. They are deciding, at least for the time being, to leave Arthur in public school. Their doctor and pastor have told them that there is nothing wrong with Arthur's mind. He knows "right from wrong" and so should have the security of discipline appropriate to his physical condition. Therefore, when he misbehaves, his TV privileges are taken away for a period of time commensurate with the seriousness of the offense. They are trying to make Ken feel that they are "family." Arthur is helping by reading to Ken.

We, here at the bottom of the canyon, are learning to look for more information about the thing that is causing our stresses. We are also examining our failures to see what can be learned from them. We are letting our friends help us. We are reading about how others handled similar problems. We are deciding what action is appropriate for each of our individual problems. Then we are acting on our decisions. Meanwhile, we thank God for the positive aspects of our experiences.

CHAPTER 6

RESPONDING TO GUILT: TRUE AND FALSE

Summary: We all make mistakes. We have accidents. If we deliberately do something that we know is wrong, then we should feel guilty. Sometimes we are forced into a situation that leaves us struggling with guilt. Michelle has to deal with guilt from such an incident. However, sometimes we feel guilty because we are not absolutely perfect. Such a feeling can destroy us. Sometimes we feel guilty but don't know why. God will help us overcome these irrational feelings of guilt. When we fail, we need the courage to begin again. This comes through forgiveness.

It is strange the apparently unrelated thoughts that are evoked here in the bottom of the canyon. Although it was resolved long ago, the question: "Did I kill my father?" and circumstances leading up to this question are replaying themselves in my memory.

The day before my twentieth birthday, I was helping my father build a house. We were working from a scaffold that summer afternoon. To get into a better position to nail something, I stepped from the scaffold onto the square of the house. About the same time, my father lost his balance, fell from the scaffold, landed on his head, crushed two vertebrae in his neck and suffered from internal bleeding. Although paralyzed, he was conscious when he arrived at the hospital and lived two days. During most of this time he was very alert and entirely rational. I asked him if he thought that when I stepped off the scaffold I had shaken it causing him to lose his balance. He said that he didn't know. Was I responsible for my father's death? It is a haunting question. How did I handle the situation? Even though it was an accident, it produced some guilt.

Sometimes I find myself demanding absolute perfection of myself, allowing no room for accidents. I make unrealistic demands of myself, not considering my human limitations. Failing to realize impossible goals, I excoriate myself and grovel in feelings of guilt. When in retrospect, I realize that I might have said or done things differently I visualize a beautiful outcome instead of being realistic. This is especially true following some trauma in my life. Often in the grieving process there are periods of feeling guilty. Most of us here at the bottom of the canyon have active imaginations about what might have been if . . . We develop real guilt trips even if they are not warranted. Have you been there also?

Michelle has joined us here in the canyon. She was a middle child. Her brother, the family favorite, was continually berating her. He would set her up: "Sis, I consider you to be the flower of the family!" only to knock her down with: "the bloomin' idiot!" Then he would laugh as her face turned red. On the other hand, her sister was the "beauty" of the family. No matter how hard Michelle tried, no one noticed her when her sister was nearby. One time when "baby sister" was two and Michelle was celebrating her fourth birthday by opening her present, a doll, the baby cried and said, "Where's mine?" After that "baby sister" received presents on two birthdays per year — hers and Michelle's. Michelle didn't.

To try to overcome the Middle Child Syndrome, Michelle started keeping the house clean at age eight. She would come in from school and clean house before she tackled her schoolwork.

While her sister sat in a soft chair and read and her brother was outside playing, Michelle would sweep and mop the floors before her mother and father got home from work. There were times when her parents didn't notice that she had done the work. But it seemed to give her life meaning. She knew that her parents loved her but they were too busy or too tired to spend quality time with her. Since she was shy, what time the parents did have was spent with her siblings.

In her early teen years she became "hooked" on country music. She wrote fan mail to a local radio "artist." She was chosen as president of his Fan Club. At last she had an identity. Even that did not make her popular in school.

Her mother and father were strict about dating rules. "No dating until you are sixteen." That year came about the time a young man returned from the Army. When this handsome twenty-five-year-old, named Andy, came back to the hometown, he noticed Michelle. Encouraged by his sister, Andy asked Michelle for a date. Flattered by the attention of an older man, Michelle accepted. It wasn't long until Andy was serious about this relationship. Michelle wasn't so sure. She tried to break it off. Andy threatened to commit suicide if she broke up with him. She began to feel guilty. She felt trapped. She didn't know what love was. He claimed to love her. She was quite certain that she didn't love him. He kept pushing the relationship – one time being gentle and another time being threatening – playing on her emotions. Each time she thought of a "way out," Andy found a way to block it. One day he proposed. She responded that she wasn't even through high school. "We can get married during the summer and then you can finish your senior year and graduate." Michelle hesitated: "It won't work." Andy promised her that he would see to it that she was allowed to finish her high school after they were married. Finally, Michelle "caved in" to the pressure. Guilt was building inside of her.

Andy and Michelle were married during the summer after her Junior year in high school. They moved to a large city so that

Andy could find work. Michelle, being accustomed to a small-town high school, was overwhelmed. The changes were too much for her — single to married, small-town to large city, friendly high school to impersonal learning factory, unpregnant to pregnant. Yes, at the end of the first year her first child was born. The next year, another son. The third year, a daughter. Three babies by the time she was twenty. She fell into a routine of taking care of babies, keeping house and preparing meals. But at least that was the last of the babies.

Life rocked on for ten years. Michelle tried to figure out what love was. "I am married to this man and I am determined to love him. I am mother to his children. I love my children. I am happy!" Michelle was homesick. She wanted to move closer to her parents. Andy was having trouble at work. With Michelle so unhappy, Andy had trouble concentrating on his job. Finally, they decided to move back to the hometown. It was not a good move. Andy couldn't find work. A compromise was worked out. They moved to another town nearby where Andy found work. They bought an old house to "fix up." They moved in before it was finished. Finally life was livable.

One day, a neighbor visited the family and invited them to church. Andy resisted. "I am disciplining my children, teaching them right from wrong and don't want them associating with those hypocrites down at church." The neighbor was kind. Her visits became a regular thing. Andy still insisted that they didn't need the church. However, Michelle began to be miserable with the load of guilt that she was carrying. Finally, she got the children ready and went to church. This became a regular routine on Sunday morning.

Shortly after that, the middle boy asked his Sunday School teacher how to become a Christian. She told him about God's love and forgiveness. "If you will admit that you have sinned and are willing to have Jesus change you, He will forgive you and make you a Christian." He prayed and suddenly the boy felt light and happy inside. He was truly changed. Even his father and mother noticed it. A few days later, Michelle talked to her pastor and he explained the "Way of Salvation" to her and she accepted Christ as her personal Savior. The other children followed. Andy continued to stubbornly resist. There were many ugly scenes where he would ridicule the "hypocrites," mock the church practices, threaten his family and damned the church and "this Christian stuff!" One Sunday morning, he disconnected the wire to the distributor so that the car would not start. Michelle and the children walked to church. They were late, but they went. That increased Andy's anger. He shouted at Michelle: "I'll move us far away from any church. Maybe then you will forget this Christian foolishness." Michelle quietly replied: "You may take me out of church but you can't take Christ out of my heart." The battle continued to rage.

The crisis came when Andy proclaimed: "I won't live with a woman who puts anyone ahead of me — not even God! I must be 'number one' in your life. Either leave God or get out." Michelle continued to let Christ be in control of her life. Andy continued to tell her to "give up this Christ stuff or get out." After a few months, Andy was at the end of his patience. He pronounced the ultimatum: "Either you give up Christianity or get out. I mean it." Michelle left.

Although Michelle did not believe in divorce she was forced to face it. Andy bribed Michelle's lawyer, who told her if she would sign "these papers" then she would have custody of the children. "But is says here that I surrender the custody of my children." "Yes, I know but this is just a form that you must sign so that we can go to court and get your children for you. I promise you!" Without knowing it, she signed away her rights to the children. Another lawyer found out about the situation and took the case back to court. The children were given their choice of whom they wanted to stay with. Andy quietly showed the children a revolver and said, "If you go with your mother, I will kill her with this gun." Of course they chose to stay with their father to protect their mother. Michelle couldn't understand because she didn't know about the gun at the time.

Now Michelle joins us in the canyon. She is depressed, has thoughts of suicide but worst of all is the feeling of guilt over her divorce. "Did I do the right thing? If I had tried harder, perhaps I could have won Andy to Christ. Should I have stayed and made him physically throw me out of the house? I have been taught all my life that divorce is wrong. Now I am guilty of being divorced. I never intended it to be. The only thing that gave me peace is now a barb in my soul. O my God, what happened?"

Is there anything in the Bible that can help us with the guilt problem? Four biblical instances come to my mind as we are working with our problem of guilt: Judas, Peter, Pilate and the chief priests.

Judas betrayed his Lord! Before you fault him too severely, have you ever been impatient with the way God was handling a problem that you talked to Him about? I don't know Judas' motivation. I only know what he did. Perhaps we can reconstruct a scenario that is a possibility. Judas was treasurer of the apostles. John said that at times he had helped himself to some of the money. Time went on and probably he became uncomfortable with the debt. An idea began to germinate in his mind. He had followed Jesus in close association for nearly three years now. He had witnessed the great power of this man. Surely He was the one to reestablish the throne of David and overthrow the Roman oppressors. But why was Jesus waiting so long? Perhaps Judas thought that he could solve both problems at the same time — recoup the money and help Jesus make up His mind to overthrow the Romans. He "went unto the chief priests, and said unto them, What will you give me, and I will deliver him unto you? And they covenanted with him for thirty pieces of silver. And from that time he sought opportunity to betray him." (Matt. 26:14-16) If Jesus were taken captive and tried by chief priests, there would be a disturbance. This conflict would come to the attention of the Romans. With such odds against Him, surely Jesus would be forced to proclaim Himself King and destroy all opposition.

Judas could then step forward and claim credit for helping in establishing the new world regime. From the perspective of history, surely this was a big mistake. True, it was premeditated, but even Judas realized that he had misread the situation. About this same time, Peter did not act in a perfect manner either. Jesus asked him and two other apostles to watch and pray with Him in the Garden of Gethsemane. They were tired and went to sleep. The Lord came and wakened them "and said unto them, Why are you sleeping? Rise and pray, lest you enter into temptation." (Luke 22:46) But they couldn't keep their eyes open. Peter had failed his Lord.

Earlier, Peter proclaimed loudly that he would remain loyal to Jesus no matter what happened. He assured his Lord that he was willing to go to prison or even die with Him. (Luke 22:33) Then came the episode in which Jesus was taken prisoner. Peter, true to his word, whipped out his sword and began to defend Him. Jesus told him to put the sword away. Peter became confused and left the garden.

Later, he decided to keep track of what was happening and entered the courtyard. In the midst of his confusion, he was confronted with the claim that he was one of Jesus' followers. He vehemently denied the accusation. On two subsequent occasions, he denied any association with Jesus, even using an oath to support his claim. As Jesus had predicted, Peter had denied Him three times before morning. When the rooster crowed, Jesus turned and looked at Peter, who suddenly became aware of what he had just done. He hurriedly left the scene. Unlike the case of Judas, this act of Peter's was not premeditated. He still experienced guilt.

Pilate was called to the court early that morning by the chief priests seeking a death warrant against some man. When he arrived, Pilate was greeted with a near riot hysteria. He had only marginal knowledge of the man that had been brought before him. Upon examining Jesus, he found Him "not guilty" and was about to release Him when the mob's cry against Jesus forced him to reconsider. While he was questioning Jesus, Pilate received word from his wife that he was in a dangerous position and should try to avoid a negative decision in this case. As a possible way out of the complicated situation, he sent Jesus to Herod for judgment. Herod found Jesus uncooperative. He would not do any magic tricks to entertain him. So Herod sent Him back to Pilate with a "not guilty of death" verdict.

When Pilate heard that Jesus claimed to be the Son of God, he tried every political maneuver that he could imagine to release Jesus. However, he did not have the courage to defy the mob and after further deliberation and attempts to free Jesus, Pilate finally succumbed to the pressure and sentenced Jesus to die. In the process, however, he showed signs of experiencing deep guilt. He was a victim of circumstances.

You probably are aware that guilt is a feeling that may or may not have a rational basis. When we knowingly and willfully violate our moral code, we should feel guilty because we are. If we habitually ignore our conscience, our moral perspicuity will be impaired and we may not feel guilty even though we are. Our minds have amazing powers of rationalization that provide "reasons" for our innocence. Sometimes when we receive new information that would require a change in our life-style or imply that our moral code is defective, it is easier to destroy the source for our needed change than to change. We often feel justi-fied in doing so.

The chief priests and elders showed no signs of guilt even when their pending action was challenged. Judas returned the money with the wail, "I have betrayed the innocent blood." To which the chief priests and elders responded, "What is that to us? See thou to that." (Matt. 27:4) The amazing rationalizing power of the mind is seen at work here. They felt no guilt because they were sure that the torture and death of Jesus was justified. The group had already held a conference and had decided on this plan of action. The session in which Jesus was "tried, in *absentia*" is described for us by John: "Then gathered the chief priests and the

Pharisees a council and said, 'What do we? for this man is doing many miracles. If we let him thus alone, all men will believe on him: and the Romans shall come and take away both our place and nation.' And one of them named Caiaphas, being the high priest that same year, said unto them, 'You know nothing at all, nor consider that it is expedient for us that one man should die for the people, and that the whole nation perish not.'" (John 11:47-50) Acts of brutality committed in the name of God seem to be the most violent.

I have read about another situation in which guilt is referred to as a complex. There is a nebulous feeling of anxiety akin to the feeling of guilt. There is no apparent cause for this feeling. It has no focus. The feeling is just as real and debilitating as guilt, but is very difficult to deal with because its underlying cause is in our subconscious.

What action can be taken to resolve the feelings of guilt? If these feelings arise from a "complex" sometimes counseling may be necessary to defuse this situation. I learned about the "guilt complex" from experience. When as a teenager, I experienced a mild case of it. When I told my mother, she asked if I was conscious of any "sin". I had not willfully violated my moral code. She then suggested that I ask God to reveal the source of this feeling or remove it. With an open heart before God, I asked in childlike faith that God would help me with this problem. Gradually the feeling disappeared.

What about the case of the "chief priests and elders"? Since they had no sense of guilt, they pursued their hate-inspired actions to conclusion. They called for Jesus' blood to be upon them and their children. (Matt 27:25) What Jesus had said to the Pharisees earlier seems to describe this situation: "They that are whole need not a physician: but they that are sick." (Luke 5:31) On another occasion: "Jesus said, 'For judgment I am come into this world, that they which see not might see; and they which see might be made blind.' And some of the Pharisees which were with him heard these words, and said unto him, 'Are we blind also?' Jesus said unto them, 'If you were blind, you should have no sin: but now you say, We see; therefore your sin remains.'" (John 9:39-41) This seems to say that if we <u>consciously</u> rationalize our actions, we are guilty of sin whether we sense it or not. If we become involved in sin unwittingly, we accrue no guilt. Jesus prayed concerning the mob which were caught up in the excitement: "Father, forgive them; for they know not what they do." (Luke 23:34)

Pilate tried to squirm his way out of the situation that made him uncomfortable. He would not face up to the responsibility that had been given him and tried to shift the blame to others. By washing his hands, he symbolically was "washing away his guilt". This tells me that if we will not accept the responsibility for our own actions in any given situation, we are not in a position to receive relief from our guilt. "The devil made me do it" is no excuse and our subconscious knows it.

Judas followed the proceedings as closely as possible. He wanted to be there when Jesus called the angels of heaven to defend Him. If he had calculated correctly, that would be a great time to step up and acknowledge the fact that he was one of the special followers of Jesus. "But what's this! Jesus is not defending Himself. He is condemned to death! Wait!! This was not in the script! This was not my plan." Judas tried to reverse his field and return the money. The chief priests and elders only laughed at him. "You struck your bargain, we got what we want, now you live with the consequences." Judas went out into the early morning light with only darkness in his heart. The forces of evil have ways of enticing you and when you yield, they laugh at your attempts to recover.

Judas had been with Jesus, but many of the lessons were not taken to heart and this proved his destruction. Had Jesus not told the story of the lost sheep? The sheep had strayed away from the flock, but the loving shepherd joyfully brought him back. Then there was the willful son that demanded his freedom. He had misread the world situation and ended up in a pig pen. When he sought restoration, he found a loving father willing to forgive. Had Judas understood these parables, and many other teachings of Jesus, he could have faced up to his guilt and found forgiveness. Instead, he was overwhelmed with despair and committed suicide.

Despair is destructive, whether it leads to physical suicide or not. Despair sees the light at the end of a tunnel as a train about to crush him. Despair falls out of an airplane and won't pull the rip-cord because the parachute probably wouldn't open anyway. Despair says that there is no use to try, any effort to remedy the situation would be wasted energy. Despair drove Michelle to the verge of suicide. She was driving his car down a long, steep hill with large trees on the side of the road. She thought: "How easy it would be to let the car gain speed to about ninety miles per hour and then 'miss the curve' near the foot of the hill. The car would be crushed against the tree and I would be free from this pain and guilt." Then she remembered that God had forgiven her before and perhaps He would remove her guilt again.

Peter also went out into the early morning light. Peter also repented of his failure. Peter faced up to the fact that he had failed his Lord in the moment of crisis. Peter faced his guilt and wept bitterly.

But there was hope! Before all this happened, in addition to the teachings of Jesus about the mercy of God, Peter remembered that "the Lord said, Simon, Simon, behold, Satan has desired to have you, that he may sift you as wheat. But I have prayed for you, that your faith fail not: and when you are converted, strengthen your brethren." (Luke 22:31,32) Jesus' prayer was that his faith fail not, but then he used the word "converted". That must have implied an expected return. Although Peter was still confused about all that was happening, he maintained his faith and hope that soon he would see the solution to this mad puzzle. In the mean-time, it felt good to cry.

Peter's hope was justified. His prayer of repentance was heard. The risen Lord had a private meeting with Peter. (Luke 24:34) His reconciliation was beginning. But this was only the beginning of the reconciliation. After the apostles left Jerusalem for Galilee, Peter's restless nature got the better of him. He went fishing and took some of his friends along. After a frustrating night in which they caught no fish, Jesus revealed Himself to them by telling them where to find the fish. Peter eagerly joined his Lord on the shore of the lake. After a good breakfast, Jesus talked straight to Peter. Evidently, forgiveness did not mean ignoring of the failure. Jesus wanted to restore Peter to a place of leadership, but first he must learn that with leadership comes responsibility.

"Peter, do you love me more than these?" (John 21:15) Casually Peter replied, "Sure." Jesus tried again with essentially the same question. "Of course, you know that I am your friend," was Peter's reply. After a pause, Jesus spoke as though he had been searching the depth of Peter's spirit: "Are you sure that you love Me as a friend?" This upset Peter. He must have remembered that Jesus had predicted that he would deny any association with Him even though Peter had staunchly denied that he would do any such thing. This time, Peter answered very carefully and thoughtfully, "Lord, You know everything. You know that I do love you."

Even as they conversed, Peter began to see what his love for Christ would cost him. He was uneasy and wanted to know if others would have to pay the same price. "What about John?" Peter then learned the most important lesson of all: Our relation to Christ is a personal relationship. The denial, the repentance, the forgiveness, and the restoration were between Peter and Christ. At last Peter had found the secret of handling guilt.

What about my father and me? Neither of us minimized the seriousness of the possibility of my involvement in the accident. As we faced the possibility together, I sensed my father's love. He did not condemn me. I was forgiven. At the time I wished that he had said, "There was no way, son." But now, I am glad that he didn't, because I have accepted my humanity and forgiven myself.

Michelle pulled off the road and stopped the car. As she

leaned over the steering wheel she asked for forgiveness. "Lord, remove this feeling of guilt for allowing my ex-husband to run me off from my children. Easy the pain of losing them. May I sense Your forgiving love." She was forgiven. However, here in the bottom of the canyon she is still having trouble forgiving herself.

Some of us at the bottom of the canyon are feeling guilt — real or imagined. It is no fun. It causes deep pain. But we are also realizing that we must hold onto the hope that is offered us by our loving Lord. When there is no evidence that we have intentionally done something that violates our moral code, we ask God, in His mercy, to remove this burden.

But when our guilt is associated with a particular action or set of circumstances for which we were responsible, we are trying not to make excuses. We have found it dangerous to consciously rationalize away our guilt. Instead, we are facing our guilt head on and seeking forgiveness. We believe that God is gracious and will forgive us when we ask Him.

But what about other people? My father forgave me. But what about Michelle's problem? Michelle has forgiven Andy, but Andy wouldn't forgive Michelle. She is trying to leave it in God's hands, accepting His forgiveness for the time being.

CHAPTER 7

FIGHTING FEAR WITH FAITH

Summary: The Bible offers us promises that can help us in fighting fear. Often times we read into the promises those things that we want them to say. When things don't turn out like we had hoped, it threatens our faith. However, faith in the goodness and wisdom of God can "cast out fear."

Please be patient with me while I reminisce about my journey through fear to faith. It all started with a phone call. — "You have cancer!" My late wife, Hattie was on the telephone and I was on the extension. Our doctor was telling us the results of the latest tests. For weeks, Hattie had been getting more and more hoarse until she could not speak above a whisper. When the various treatments of the symptoms had failed, the doctor had ordered an x-ray. The x-ray indicated that there was something abnormal in her chest. The doctor checked it to see if possibly it was an aneurism. I saw the x-ray. The mass was reticular. I suspected cancer, but kept the horrible thought to myself. Now, after a biopsy of a nearby lymph node, the diagnosis was definite.

The pronouncement came as a death sentence. Could this be happening to us? Cancer was something that happened only to the other fellow. Unless you have heard those dreadful words, you have no idea how devastating the shock and penetrating the fear can be. After the doctor gave us advice and tried the shore up our sagging feelings, he finished the conversation and hung up the phone.

Hattie came back into the bedroom where I was and we both sat on the bed, huddled in shock. Somewhere from the depths of my memory came the words, "Fear thou not for I am with thee: be not dismayed for I am thy God: I will strengthen thee; yea, I will help thee, yea, I will uphold thee with the right hand of my righteousness." (Isaiah 41:10) Hattie grasped these words. She claimed them as her own. These words had broken the spell and now she was ready to plan for the future.

"We will go to Birmingham to the University Hospital connected with the Medical Center. They will run more test to determine the extent, verify the kind of cancer and specify the treatment." She was encouraging me: "We'll make it, Honey!"

Frankly, what does that Scripture say to you? Doesn't it call to mind the times when you were small and you brought you fears and hurts to your father or mother and they took you in their arms, kissing the hurts and making them well? Didn't that Promise mean that the tests would be definitive, God would miraculously make the cancer go away, and further tests establish that Hattie was clear of cancer? It seemed a wonderful way to bring glory to Himself.

Well, we went to Birmingham. The tests were run. The results were ambiguous. The doctors decided that she should be admitted to the hospital and have a laparotomy. They removed her spleen, gall-bladder, and appendix. They took sample tissues from nearly everything else in her abdomen. The good news came back — no cancer there. Wonderful! A couple of less serious surgeries did not satisfy the doctors. They decided to open her chest and get at the offending tumor. When they did, they found the cancer, as expected, but because of the location surrounding an important nerve, they could only remove samples of the tissue. In the meantime, I was teaching class in the morning, driving the 130 miles to the hospital in the afternoon, returning home in the evening to check on my three daughters, the oldest of whom was seventeen. Hattie was worried about me. My hair was turning white. Radiation therapy was planned. What had happened to the *Deus ex machina* promise?

Hattie endured all the operations, the trauma and embarrassment of radiation therapy with remarkable courage. She continually thought of others, especially her family. In the midst of all this, she prayed for ten more years of reasonable health that she might finish the job of raising her family to the point that they could be independent.

Would she ever talk again? The doctors would not venture a guess. In time, the nausea stopped, the radiation burns healed and the hair grew back on the upper part of her neck. Later, she gradually got her voice back. God had answered prayer and kept His promise. With each check-up, our faith grew. As I related in chapter one, we returned to Birmingham monthly, quarterly, then every six months, until we finally crossed the "magic" five-year mark. The doctors had said that if she remained clear of cancer for five years, then she was past the danger zone. Six years passed, and things began to take on an air of normalcy. Seven years after the radiation, the doctor asked me to come into the office with Hattie. He showed us the x-ray and there was more trouble. "Perhaps it is just a lesion, but we need to know for sure." This meant another operation in which they opened her chest and went to the source of the trouble.

Where was God's promise now? It was time to read it again. The amazing thing is that it didn't say what we wanted it to say or what we thought that it had said. At first glance, I thought it said that we would experience no trauma, no significant pain, and that the present difficulty was an illusion. Then as the facts began to confirm the doctor's diagnosis, I thought that this would only be a temporary problem. That God would heal her and thus bring glory to His name and strength to our faith.

The next level of interpretation was that we would be able to understand the reason for this illness and then Hattie would be completely cured bringing honor to the power and wisdom of God. This experience would enhance our ability to minister to others. It would give us insight into the mystery of God's greatness. It would help us to see clearly how God interacts with the human scene. As it turned out, Hattie "sat with" a friend who was hospitalized with cancer. Instead of her experience enhancing her ministry, it brought back vividly all the horror of the cancer experience.

As things progressed, we read this scripture again and behold it didn't even promise that we would be conscious of God's presence. It simply says "I am with thee." However, it continues, "They that war against thee shall be as nothing; they that strive with thee shall perish." This seemed to say that ultimately Hattie would win the fight against cancer.

If we observe this world objectively, it would appear to be inherently evil — opposed to the ultimate good. Cruelty is visible everywhere. It would appear from the second law of thermodynamics that if it is a closed system, it is spontaneously degenerate. (Falling apart.) Jesus indicated that devil was the "ruler of this world". (John 12:31) This would support the observation that we live in a hostile environment. This would give us cause to fear except for the fact that God is the final authority.

Hattie was not one to underline her Bible very much. After her death, I found several verses underlined in Isaiah 40 through 44. This prompted me to read our special promise in its context. This helped me to understand that I had been misinterpreting these promises.

The prophet is writing to a group of people that had thought that being God's Chosen people meant that they were invincible. Even after the Northern Kingdom of Israel was carried away into captivity by the Assyrians, the Southern Kingdom thought that they would be exempt from that kind of sorrow. Then it happened! The Babylonians captured the Holy City, carried most of the people back to slavery in Babylon. Now years had passed and the people had become accustomed to their new environment.

Into the situation marched a new military leader who seemed invincible. The whole civilized world seemed to be crumbling around them. Fear gnawed at the heart of everyone. Did God have a message to this people whose faith had been badly shaken by events that had taken place and the frightening chaos that the future seemed to hold?

The prophet came with the message: "Comfort ye my people." (Isaiah 40:1) "Fear not . . ." appears at least seven times in chapters 41-44. Those of us who have been disappointed when things did not turn out the way we had planned them need to reread these scriptures and realize the human tendency to interpret what we read according to our bias.

The text really says, "Fear thou not for I am with thee. . ." In retrospect, I realize that Hattie believed that. Her courage was amazing to all our friends. She did not enjoy the suffering. One day a friend of mine spoke about Hattie's spirit in the face of her difficulties, and said that she would have a special "crown" in heaven because of the way she was "carrying such a heavy cross" here. When I told her, she joked: "I would be willing to have a less elaborate crown there if it meant a lighter burden here." Through it all, though, that is the closest that she ever came to complaining.

For the most part, she was not afraid. Only twice during the thirteen years of her fight did I see her afraid. Once when I was sick, she obviously was afraid that she could not manage life if I died first. The other time was the night that she was temporarily paralyzed and could not move her hand to ring the bell to alert me of her trouble. Miraculously, I heard her call me and when I rushed into the room, I could sense that she was afraid.

"Be not dismayed, for I am thy God. . ." To be dismayed is to be so overcome by fear that you cannot think clearly. Hattie's mind was not paralyzed by fear. In fact, after the doctor's announcement, and our claiming the promise, I was more irrational than she. She was the one who calmed me and outlined a plan of action. Until three days before her death, she was completely rational and expressed her love for her family and others. She did say after she became paralyzed from the neck down that she thought that I would need to learn to iron my shirts and get my supper.

"I will strengthen thee . . ." It is amazing the stamina that Hattie had. One time when she was in the middle of a chemotherapy regimen, she experienced intense chest pains. I called the hospital in Birmingham and was told that she could come the next day. I doubted that she would be able to make the trip, but she insisted on trying it. Even though we waited in the waiting room for more than an hour sitting up uncomfortable chairs, she had strength to do what was needed.

She had considerable neuropathy as a result of chemotherapy. It was not completely reversible. When she was having the most trouble with her walking, the doctor suggested a walker. I purchased one and brought it home to her. She learned to use it, but when I wasn't looking, she would take about six or eight steps in rapid succession and then plunk the walker down, leaning on it to rest a while before she made another dash. Such was her impatience with being disabled. God had given her strength.

After some chemotherapy, she went back to work when she was so weak that she had to support herself by "leaning" on the wall with her hands, using hand over hand, walk down the hall to her desk. In spite of her illness and treatment, she had very few absences from work. God gave her strength.

The last week in April, she took her first trip without me since we had married. She flew to Oklahoma City to help our oldest daughter, Joan, prepare for her wedding. This was a hectic time with a considerable stress. Yet, when I arrived by automobile about a week later, she had strength enough to hug me! God had remembered His promise.

About a year before her death, she made a trip to Mobile, Alabama with me. She had suffered from significant weakness when she walked. While we were in Mobile, we wanted to see the Bellingrath Gardens. When we arrived, we found we could not see them from any vehicle, but only from a foot-path. It was over a mile of walking and would probably necessitate Hattie's being on her feet for over an hour. She wanted to try! God kept His promise and strengthened her for this delightful experience. The next day, she passed out from being on her feet long enough to answer the door to the motel room.

The next summer, our son, Don, bought a house in Colorado Springs. He wanted us to help him move, buy furniture, put up some extra shelves, fix the drapes, and little extra touches that make a house a home. My youngest daughter, Julia, and I planned to go out to help him. We wanted Hattie to plan to go. As the time drew near, she realized that she could not make it, but insisted that she could take care of herself. We went, but kept the phone lines busy checking on Hattie. It worked out o.k. We did most of the things that were necessary except for the drapes and little things that needed a mother's touch.

In December of that year, about four months before Hattie's death, I was supposed to fly to Denver to attend a conference. Miraculously, Hattie thought that she might have strength enough to make the trip. We planned in that direction. The time came, we drove to Huntsville, climbed the stairs into the plane, flew to Denver, walked (she refused to allow me to get a wheelchair) the whole length of that long concourse in Stapleton Airport, rented a car, and drove to Colorado Springs. Hattie did not even go to bed immediately when we arrived. That week, I commuted to the conference, but the amazing thing is that Hattie shopped in the evening, worked on the house during the day, and then shopped for more supplies that evening so that she could work the next day on making Don's house a home. For an entire week, she had only one bad day. She made the trip home without any significant trouble. Once again, God had kept His promise.

"I will help thee . . ." The next month, we made a trip to Birmingham to the hospital. While we were there, it began to snow. In the North that was never a big deal, but in the South it is something to dread. It was late in the evening before we could start home. The roads were wet and it was still snowing, but there seemed to be no imminent danger. About 65 miles from home, the snow was covering the roads. As I came out from the lee of one bridge, the wind caught the car and slid it sideways a few inches. Hills, curves, bridges lay between us and home. As we passed one danger point, Hattie said, "Thank the Lord and now let's pray that the Lord will help us over the Elk River bridge." And so it was the rest of the way home. We live on a hill with a rather steep approach to our driveway. Our drive has a large oak tree on one side and a retaining wall on the other. That night, we were able to park our car in our own driveway. Once again, God had kept His promise.

During one of the final chemotherapy regimens, the doctors injected methetrexate into Hattie's spinal fluid. This powerful poison left Hattie weak. I wanted to save her strength and so we stayed at a nearby hotel over night, returning home the next day. As we left the hospital the third time that she received this treatment Hattie said, "Let's go home." We did. She made the trip successfully. She had been "upheld by God's right hand." In retrospect, I think about the journey. Premature death has always been a problem for me. Death by accident or disease has raised disturbing questions. When someone whom we love dearly dies prematurely, these questions threaten our faith. The "why" thrusts its barbs deep into our hearts. However, looking at the life of Christ, we see a person who died prematurely, though innocent. He died because of sin – not His own sin but because He became a member of the human species and sin is a part of the fabric of our present existence. Perhaps all premature deaths are due to sin – not necessarily personal sin but "corporate" sin. When sin entered the human race as a result of free choice, God drove the primordial couple from the garden lest they eat from the tree of life. (Genesis 3:24) This indicates that physical death is a direct result of sin. It would appear that Enoch and Elijah are examples of God's original plan.

Death is an enemy, but I have observed that fear of death can be conquered by faith in God. A foundation for this faith is the resurrection of Jesus and His promise that: "Because I live, ye shall live also." (John 14:19) Hattie did not want to die. She fought death successfully for many years. Ultimately, however, she was not afraid to die.

One of the greatest threats to faith is reading into the Bible those things that we want to read. The problem is not new and is not limited to a few. I have learned that God does keep His promises, but not always in the way we interpret them.

Many times people are cruel in their accusations that a person who is sick or dies, lacks faith. In the "faith" chapter of the Bible, the author details many exploits that were accomplished because of faith but he also tells of others tortured, destitute, afflicted, and tormented. He states that these also "obtained a good report through faith. . ." (Hebrews 11:35-39)

Sarah has another approach to faith. When she lost her job, she faced her fears. She has been praying a lot lately, even while looking for a job. Of course, she is reading her Bible, but spends much of her day in private prayer. She says that she has "prayed through" and is no longer afraid. In fact, she seems to be eagerly waiting to see how her Lord is going to solve this problem. We were surprised, although she wasn't, when she was reading the paper and found an ad for someone to share a house. When she went to investigate, it was a widow with a teenage son who wanted to have someone share the house and help pay the rent. (Half of the rent for the whole house is much less than she is paying for one room with kitchen privileges.) It was arranged for Sarah and Mike to move in and start paying half of the rent as soon as Sarah finds employment. She is going to be able to get her belongings out of storage, move in, and start making a home for Mike again. Needless to say, her faith is strong. In spite of Sarah's success in dealing with part of her problem, we are finding that faith is not the magic carpet to mystery land. It is not the pursuit of one's willful way with the aid of a divine genie. Sarah acknowledges that.

Another problem is arising. It appears that all this uncertainty in Sarah and Mike's life has taken its toll on Mike's schoolwork. It now appears certain that he will fail English and so cannot graduate from the eighth grade. The irony of it is that he is scheduled to sing in the graduation exercises. The class still wants him to sing "I'm Sitting On Top of the World." If Sarah can find employment in time, he can take English in Summer School and move on with his class. But that is a big if!

Jim and Susie have patiently listened to my discussion of the "promise" and its evolving interpretation. They sit pensively for a while and then begin to tell their story.

Jim supplements his Bible reading with the lyrics of the songs of the church. He has always had an interest in music and gains comfort and inspiration in singing. One song that has been his "promise" is: "He Never Has Failed Me Yet." The song talks about the journey of life passing through valleys dark and deep, through the "heat of the day" and foes and ills that we encounter but through it all, Jesus has never failed us. Therefore, we can face the future with confidence that He will not fail us. It has now been five years since Arthur was diagnosed. The prognosis was probably a maximum of six years. Next year is pressing the limit. How can they make this year the most meaningful?

Betty, Susie's mother, is having considerable trouble with Arthur's illness. It seems that recently she was scheduled for surgery for ulcers. On Friday, her pastor came and talked with her and then prayed for her healing. God answered immediately. Before the surgery on Monday, they did a final test to determine the extent of the surgery that would be necessary and found that her ulcers had completely healed. So she discussed Arthur's problem with her pastor. After the whole problem was clear, she asked him to pray with her for Arthur's healing. They prayed together. Faith soared. God is good! But Arthur got worse.

Arthur and Ken are staying with Betty, their grandmother, after schools until one of their parents get home from work. During the first week of school it is becoming clear that Arthur is not managing well. He can handle his homework fine. But something is wrong. It is becoming clear that Arthur cannot maneuver around the school any more. He falls too frequently even when walking on a smooth, uncluttered floor. Not only is it embarrassing but he is in danger of hurting himself.

With Arthur's worsening condition, it appears that a wheelchair is a necessity. It is true that he has made friends who are willing to push him in his wheelchair from one class to another and help out in other ways when he is in school. But succumbing to the use of a wheelchair is like admitting defeat. Arthur has fought so gallantly. "Is Jesus failing us now?"

Only too soon Arthur is going to need constant care. Betty would love to do it, but Arthur is too heavy for her to lift and besides that, Betty's health is failing. What are some other options? Put Arthur in a home? "No way!" Hire an LPN to look after him while Jim and Susie are at work? "Can't afford it. The cost of the nurse is more than Susie makes." Although Jim has a good job, but it will be nearly impossible to get along on his salary alone. The only option that is halfway acceptable is for Susie to take care of Arthur. Susie will quit her job. "How will we manage?" They pray about it, presenting their dilemma to the Lord. They have a peace about it. "We believe that Jesus will provide someway. He has not failed us in the past and we hold confidently to the hope that He will not fail us now! We rest in that confidence."

Then another specter appears to haunt Betty. "What if Arthur dies before I do? I don't think that I can take it!" She continues to spend time with her grandson, even spoils him a bit. The more that she thinks about it, the more difficult it becomes to her. However, she never considers denouncing God. Just pleads with Him to let her die first. It is a distinct possibility because she is not in good health.

Isabelle is afraid of falling back into the pit of clinical depression. The emotional pain is nearly unbearable. Is there any way out? Is suicide an option? At this point she does not have a particular biblical promise or a special hymn to encourage her. Her counselor encourages her to believe that there is hope for the future. "There will be an end of hurting. God knows what you need and will provide it in His own time." For the time being, that is enough to hold on to. She trusts her counselor.

Michelle is facing many problems. She has saved a little money, but that won't go far unless she finds a job and a place to live. More important is finding a reason to live. She is on her own because of her refusal to give up her Christian faith. Will that faith provide for her in this time of need? She can only trust. Surely her Christ will not fail her now.

Faith is trust in the goodness and wisdom of God. Faith can cast out fear. It is working for us.

CHAPTER 8

SURMOUNTING WORRY

Summary: Worry is a habit. Although the Apostle Paul had much to worry about, he gives us a "formula" that should minimize or eliminate worry. If we pray specifically and with thanksgiving, God's peace will protect our hearts and we can relax in God's will.

It looks as though there is one last obstacle to face before we plan our escape from this canyon, namely, worry. Worry has always been a bit of a problem for me, but since my "fall" it has become a real problem.

The shock of Hattie's death depressed my worry button and it became stuck in the "on" position. However, I was not aware of that immediately. A few months after my wife's death, Julia, my youngest daughter, asked my advice about attending the National Council of Teachers of Mathematics convention in Washington, D.C. I thought that with plenty of lead-time, she would get a room in the primary convention hotel. I encouraged her to go. When her reservations came back, she was assigned a hotel in downtown Washington several miles from the convention site. My worry alarm went off! Julia trusts nearly everyone taking him or her at face value. I felt that D.C. was not the place for such a trusting young lady. I still urged her to go because it would help her professionally, but deep inside, I worried. I asked her to call me every night after she returned to her room. The conference went very well and she returned home safely. Thank God!

Shortly after this, my oldest daughter told me that she was expecting. Worry began to take control again. The worry button was still stuck. I visualized all the things that could go wrong: the child could be physically handicapped, could be mentally retarded, could be stillborn or Joan could die giving birth. Other problems came to mind. I have a very active imagination — all bad. About eight months later, I received a phone call at 2:45 a.m. Jim's message was: "It's a boy and everybody is o.k." He is a man of few words, but at that time of the morning that was all I needed to hear. Since that time the pediatrician continues to declare him to be a healthy baby boy.

Others of those at the bottom of the canyon with me admit that worry is a problem for them. They worry about being rejected, about being alone, about contracting a life-threatening illness, about failing, about getting old or dying before they get old, about money or other contingencies. After a fall such as each of us has had, we seem to be especially vulnerable.

We know that we need to do something about the problem, but what can we do? We could accept as true that our worry caused everything to turn out all right. In other words that worry works. They tell us of a man who stuck carrots into his ears to keep wild elephants away. When he was told that there was not a wild elephant within 100 miles, he replied, "Effective! Isn't it?"

We could adopt the attitude that it is human to worry. Fate has decreed that some of us have a high worry-quotient. There is nothing that we can do about our worry habit. "Whatever will be, will be!" We must accept it as part of our lots in life.

As far as I am concerned, these are not acceptable solutions. Trying to solve the problem, I remember reading what Paul has written to the Philippians. He expressed a neat little "formula" that can help us attack the worry problem. It prescribes: "In nothing be anxious, but in everything by prayer and petition with thanksgiving bring all your requests into the Presence of God and the peace that is beyond understanding will constantly guard your hearts and minds in Christ Jesus." (Philippians 4:6-7).

Would you agree that our lives are complicated and that there are no simple solutions? Even so, I seek "yes or no" answers to all of life's problems. Most of our reactions to life's situations are from habit. Much of our worry is a result of habit. As with any habit, one application of the above "formula" will probably not bring the level of peace that is desired. But undesirable habits can be replaced by better habits. That is what this passage suggests about worry. Instead of worrying about everything, make it a habit to pray earnestly and thankfully about the problem in detail, and the peace of God will replace your spirit of agitation and give you rest in your inner self as you trust in Christ Jesus. "We'll try it!"

Did Paul have anything to worry about? (Anxiety and its derivatives have many connotations. In this context, I am interpreting the word in one of its weaker meanings: worry.) Consider his circumstances.

Paul was in prison. (Philippians 1:13). He was not in control of his life and his environment. Up to this time, the record of his life was one of action. He enjoyed his freedom. He exercised his privilege as a Roman citizen. His actions heretofore were constrained only by the love of Christ. (2 Corinthians 5:14). Now he was confined.

Have you ever been snowbound, quarantined, or forced to stay indoors for a while? I recall the winter of 1985 when we had nine inches of ice (dense enough to support an automobile) in North Alabama. Conditions were so hazardous that a person would receive a ticket if he or she was driving without a verifiable emergency. Most people became fidgety. Hattie was sick in bed and needed medicine. Fortunately, I was able to walk to the nearest pharmacy and get the medicine. "But what if the electricity goes off? We have no other source of heat. We won't be able to cook our food. The frozen food will spoil if I can't find an ice chest to put it in with the ice from outside. If I put it outside on the ice, maybe the animals will ruin it. What if the roof caves in? Many buildings have already collapsed under the weight of the ice. What if Hattie gets worse and needs to get to the hospital? Her doctor is in Birmingham about 130 miles away. Besides, we are pretty well stuck inside this house. Cabin fever?" Generally speaking, though, things were out of my control. Maybe that is a little bit of what Paul felt.

Paul saw one of his best friends become so sick that he was afraid that the man would die. (Philippians 2:25-30). Epaphroditus had been sent to Rome by the Phillipians to help Paul during his imprisonment. Paul reports that Epaphroditus stayed on the job even at the risk of his own life. It looked as though he would die from illness.

There was a chance that while Paul was in prison that his work would be undermined. He might have lived and died in vain. (Philippians 1:15-18). There were Paul's ever-present enemies continually trying to destroy Paul's influence. They attacked his personality, his message, his methods and his credentials. Maybe now that he was in prison they would succeed. It seemed they worked in nearly every church, but especially in the Galatian churches. He told of his earlier trip to Jerusalem to have the gospel that he preached checked for orthodoxy. He wrote, "Lest by any means I should run or have run in vain." (Galatians 2:2). At this time there were some who claimed to be preaching the same gospel that Paul preached but motivated by a quarrelsome spirit, "supposing to add affliction to my bonds," he judged. (Philippians1:16)

Paul faced death himself. (Philippians1:21-24). He had faced death before. He was stoned and left for dead in Lystra. He "fought with beasts at Ephesus." (1 Corinthians 15:32). He had been mobbed in Jerusalem only to be rescued from death by Roman soldiers. He was shipwrecked and later bitten by a poisonous snake on the way to Rome. (Acts 27,28). And now it looked as though it might go either way when he was brought to trial.

There was also a chance that Paul would slip for the faith. He said, "So fight I, not as one that beats the air: but I keep under my body, and bring it into subjection: lest that by any means, when I have preached to others, I myself should be a castaway." (1 Corinthians 9:26-27).

Another worry was that he would be alone, cold, and mentally stagnated as a result of his imprisonment. He had left his cloak at Troas, winter was approaching, his friend Trophimus was sick and had to be left behind, his books and parchments were probably with Carpus, and only Luke was with him. (2 Timothy 4:10-21). Although this was probably another imprisonment, yet these worries could well have been present as he wrote to his friends at Philippi.

What do people worry about today? We have a representative group here. One of my daughters developed a problem of excessive bleeding every month. Then her abdomen began to swell. Since her mother had died of cancer, we worry that this is cancer. Jim and Susie are facing a problem of how they can manage financially when Susie is forced to quit work in order to take care of Arthur. Also, Betty is worrying about possibly outliving Arthur. After all, this is his last year according to the prognosis. Sarah is concerned about finding a job. She is also worried about Mike, especially about his failing in school. "What will that do to his psychological development?" Larry still loves Cynthia and is worried about her welfare. She has moved to another city about 150 miles away. He will not contact her because she wanted her freedom and he will respect that desire, but he is still concerned. Isabelle is afraid of falling back into the pit of clinical depression. Her struggle is very real. Michelle is worried about being alone. She needs courage to move ahead but she is afraid of further rejection.

According to the "formula," everything is to be brought into the Presence of God. There is nothing to be hidden from God. But we sometimes like to think that we can hide from Him any thing in our lives that would make us uncomfortable in His Presence. Sometimes we are ashamed of some of our thoughts. We may feel guilty about worrying. We may be afraid to level with God because in the secret recesses of our heart we don't really trust Him. We have the notion that anything that we would genuinely like, God is against our having it. But I have found that for my praying to be effective, I must acknowledge even the things that embarrass me. — There can be no forbidden topics, no sham or fake piety, no self-justification in conversing with God.

Paul's secret "formula" further says that we are to pray about the things that trouble us. Some types of praying make us feel worse. Some prayers are simply a recital of our troubles and thereby reinforce our negative feelings about the things that are troubling us. For example, Sarah could pray like this: "Dear Lord, I am out of work because I was fired for something that was not my fault. I was never told how to handle a call to the 'big boss.' So I am now out of a job. I have tried to find work but no one will hire me. I must be too old. Of course, I now have a place to move to, but what happens if I can't find a job. That widow woman cannot continue to pay the rent all by herself. Besides, probably she won't like me when she gets to know me better. Maybe Mike and her teenage son can't get along. Lord, what am I going to do? In Jesus name, amen."

Instead, she prayed: "Our loving heavenly Father, this is your daughter. I am glad that I am Yours because I know that You are in control of my situation. I don't understand why I lost my job so abruptly, but I am confident that You know what I need. I need some means of supporting Mike and myself. My resources are limited but Yours are limitless. I thank You for providing us with a place to stay. I will still keep looking for work and I ask Your guidance in that endeavor. I am confident that You will provide for our needs. Thank You for hearing my prayer. I love You. In Jesus name, amen."

There are three aspects of effective praying that Paul suggests here. I did a little word study. This is what I found. The first word that is translated "prayer" in the King James Version, (KJV) usually denotes an attitude of worship. Many of the great prayers that are recorded for us begin with mention of the greatness of God. Solomon prayed, "Lord God of Israel, there is no God like Thee in heaven above or on the earth beneath, who keeps covenant and mercy with Thy servants that walk before Thee with all their heart. . ." (1 Kings 8:23). Hezekiah prayed, "O Lord God of Israel, which dwells between the cheribims, Thou art the God, even Thou alone, of all the kingdoms of the earth; Thou hast made heaven and earth. . . ." (2 Kings 19:15). Daniel prayed, "O Lord, the great and dreadful God, keeping the covenant and mercy to them that love Him and to them that keep His commandments . . ." (Daniel 9:4). Paul prayed, ". . . Father of our Lord, Jesus Christ, of whom the whole family in heaven and earth is named. . . ." (Ephesians 3:14-15). Jesus taught His followers to pray, "Our Father, Who art in heaven, Hallowed be Thy name. . . ."(Matthew6:9).

Too often my prayers are hurried. I rush into the Presence of God as I might visit a neighbor to borrow a cup of flour while I am making biscuits. It doesn't work well. Effective praying that helps heal the worrying spirit starts with a recognition of Who God is. Reverence is often in short supply in our lives. We will continue to worry if we think of God as "our good buddy in the skies." We need to have confidence in His wisdom and goodness.

The second aspect of praying that is denoted in the word translated in the KJV as "supplication". It implies an expression of personal need. This is the specific expression of the things that are worrying us: spelling out in particular what is and why it is bothering us. This suggests that we know what we are worrying about. If we are bothered by a general feeling of uneasiness, this aspect of prayer will help us to clarify the cause of our queasy spirit.

The third aspect of prayer is thanksgiving. This is the key. If we can bring sincere thanksgiving into my prayer, we are well on our way to peace. If the "formula" breaks down, it is usually at this point. Thanksgiving reminds us of the times in the past the God definitely heard and answered our prayers. Sarah can thank God for answering her prayer for a place to stay. This is the recent past. Also, she can thank God that she found work so soon after her husband died. I can thank God for taking care of my daughters — Julia and Joan — when I was worried about them. Betty can thank God that she has had at least five years to enjoy her grandson. Isabelle can thank God that she is making the progress that she is and for the support of her family. Jim and Susie have been able to manage in the past in spite of medical expenses and that should help build their faith. Michelle can thank God for her courage to hold on to her Christian faith against opposition from her husband and many of her family. God gave her strength then and will not forsake her now.

Sometimes when we pray about problems, we suggest solutions. Later we realize that our short-sighted solutions that were denied us, were not the best for us or others concerned. Then we thank God for "unanswered prayer." Thankfulness emphasizes the goodness of God. It builds our faith. As we recite incidents in the past in which God made the difference, we become more aware of the nature of God and how He interacts with us as humans.

How can we break the worry cycle and express thanksgiving when our hearts is so disturbed? It is not easy. The thing that I have found helpful is to start by "praying" the prayers of the Psalmist. For example, "Bless the Lord, O my soul, and all that is within me bless His holy name. Bless the Lord, O my soul, and forget not all His benefits." (Psalm 103:1-2). The words of hymns or sacred songs, such as "All Hail the Power of Jesus Name" or "O For a Thousand Tongues To Sing", are often helpful too. You may not feel the words that you are expressing at first, but after you "prime the pump," then the gratitude can flow from your heart.

The promised result of this kind of action is that the peace of God will guard our lives. I wondered what the peace of God is like. I am finding that it is internal. The peace of God does not depend on my environment. Jesus, God in the flesh, demonstrates this for us. He lived in a country in which there was a fierce loyalty to the nation of Israel. Even though the Romans had conquered the country and exacted taxes from the people, they had not captured the people's hearts. There is considerable evidence that Joseph had died leaving Jesus with the responsibility for his family at an early age by the standards of the day. His family did not have much in material possessions. He started His ministry with a heavy sense of mission, having determined the direction that He would go during a forty day fast in the wilderness area. He was to represent God to the people. After He left this earth, His ministry must not die. He must select strong leaders that would carry on the work. He selected twelve for the task. One turned traitor. All fled under pressure, although one returned to watch during the fake trial. Certainly He experienced life's pressures at their worst. Yet He was able to maintain His composure under the worst of circumstances, even when, earlier, the people tried to force Him to be their king.

At times I have confused peace with surface emotion. Jesus could distinguish between the surface emotions and the constant, abiding peace of God. For example, on one occasion, when He was in the synagogue on the Sabbath day, there was a man there that was handicapped. Jesus asked the man to stand up so that everyone could see his "withered hand". Then Jesus asked if those present thought that it would be acceptable to heal this man on the Sabbath. The consensus was that the man should stay crippled as far as they were concerned. Jesus adrenaline flowed and He became angry. (Mark 3:1-5). This surface emotion did not mean that He had lost the peace of God. On another occasion He returned to Bethany to grieving sisters. When He visited the grave of Lazarus He wept so openly and unashamedly that everyone in the crowd knew it. Some even commented on it. (John 11: 35-36). It seems obvious that the peace of God does not make you impervious to the fluctuating emotions that are common to mankind.

The peace of God is dependable. It is based on the faithfulness of God. We can see evidence of the reliability of God in nature. If the physical world were capricious, there could be no science. In science we look for patterns. This implies some regularity or reliability. As it is, we can make predictions based on past observations. When I release an object, I expect it to fall down. I have not been disappointed yet! It gives me a sense of stability to know that I can expect certain results when I have met the conditions.

Fundamentally, the peace of God comes as a result of having an integrated personality. James says, "The double-minded man is unstable in all his ways." (James 1:8). Just so, there cannot be any deep-seated peace unless there is stability in our lives. When you commit yourself completely to God, He will destroy the sin-principle that divides your loyalty. This will integrate your personality with Christ as the center thus giving you peace.

The peace of God will be a garrison for your heart and mind to ward off any attempted invasion by disturbing circumstances. Your mind represents the rational part of your personality. If you have peace of mind, you can think clearly. You can use all your intellectual power effectively in trying to find solutions to the problems facing you. The focus of your attention can be on the positive. The heart represents your central emotions. When you have peace of heart, you can remain calm and have courage in the face of threatening circumstances and a hostile environment. These things will tend to thwart worry.

All this is contained in Paul's little "formula." Does this work in the twentieth century? This year Julia went to the National Council of Teachers of Mathematics convention in Anaheim, California. She is still the trusting young lady that she always was. She allowed a young man that she met on the plane to transport her to her hotel from the Orange County airport. (He had Alaska license plates on his car.) In spite of this, I can honestly say that my worry level was lower this year.

This summer she flew to Lebanon, New Hampshire where she presented her thesis for her master's degree to her advisors at Dartmouth College. She rented a car and traveled around New England. I was practically worry free.

Later in the summer, I went to Santa Fe, New Mexico to participate in a challenging workshop. Logically, I should have worried.

Most of the other participants were from prestigious universities in the Ivy League or some big government organization, for example the National Institute of Health. I asked my Sunday School class to pray for me. I was worry free about this challenge.

Larry, realizing that he cannot change the Cynthia's situation, has committed her well-being to the God in prayer. He thanked God for the good years that they had together. As he lingered in the attitude of prayer, the Holy Spirit came to him with the assurance that his prayer had been heard. He now has a peace about the situation.

It seems to be working for us. We admit that sometimes we are having difficulty in satisfying the conditions. In that case we end up worrying. None of us has completely licked the habit. But we are all in a better state of mental health because we are trying to apply it to our lives. I confess — I don't fully understand how it works, but then "it surpasses human knowledge!" We recommend it. Why not learn along with us?

PART II

ENDURING DIFFICULTIES
PATIENTLY
COMING OUT OF THE CANYON

CHAPTER 9

ACKNOWLEDGING SOME DANGEROUS MISTAKES

Summary: Some of the mistakes that we made in dealing with life and death:

1. Some of us ignored our botany lesson.
2. Some of us wore a hat that was too big for us.
3. Some of us manufactured idols.
4. Some of us were guilty of digital thinking in an analog world
5. Some of us carried a good luck charm.
6. We thought that we could see, but we were blind.

It is now time to start our climb out of the canyon. Are you ready? I warn you that it has been my experience that the first part of the trail is rather steep. It consists of acknowledging our mistakes. Try to list yours as we recite some of ours.

"Comfort ye!" I felt like I needed comfort. My wife's death had left me with questions, that in all my years as a minister, I never knew existed. I turned to Isaiah 40 and started reading. "Comfort ye, comfort ye my people, saith your God." I continued to read through chapter 44 fascinated to realize some of the mistakes in my thinking that were being revealed to me.

First we need to be aware of the historical backdrop against which this prophecy was being enacted. The prophet was addressing a people that had been very aware of their "preferred nation" status. They had been accustomed to preferential treatment because of their God. But suddenly their world had fallen apart. The northern part of the nation was captured and dispersed by the Assyrians. The southern part of the divided nation survived longer but they too were eventually captured, their capital city razed, their temple destroyed and most of the people were taken to Babylon to form a colony there. The old generation died off and the new generation was becoming accustomed to its environment when there appeared on the horizon a fierce warrior that seemed invincible. It appeared that once again they were about to be pushed back down into the canyon. The only thing that they expected was trouble.

I can identify with these people. I had been blessed in many ways. My wife had been loving and kind. My children did things that made us proud. They loved us and we loved them. Some people had thought that I had a "hot-line to heaven." It appeared to others that we led a "charmed" life. Then cancer struck! Some of our "friends" started avoiding us. Some accused us publicly of lack of faith or secret sin. We learned to appreciate Job's situation. After radiation therapy, things settled down into a more or less acceptable routine. Then cancer struck again. After a few years, Hattie died!

Isabelle can identify with them also. Her parents were leaders in the local church. This gave her a "favored person" status in the church. She used this to help her develop her leadership skills. When she went to college, she followed her sister. Her sister's record had prepared the way for Isabelle to make friends, take the classes she wanted and to find her way around the community. There was a thread of continuity in her life. Upon graduation, she was able to move in to the apartment with her sister. Her life seemed charmed. She had a job, a place to live, some "built-in" friends and training that made her feel useful in helping others.

Then her mother died. The disorientation that was caused by this traumatic event brought her face to face with some of her limitations including her own mortality.

In this context, Isabelle and I made a mistake. WE IGNORED OUR BOTANY LESSON. It seems now as though, until then, we had forgotten that we are mortal. I had come to expect that my life with Hattie would never end in death. The marriage vows contained the phrase, "until death us do part", but that would always be in the future. Isabelle acted on the unconscious assumption that the continuity in her life would continue forever. We should have remembered what the prophet said: "All flesh is grass, and all the goodliness thereof is as the flower of the field: . . . The grass withereth, the flower fadeth: but the word of our God shall stand forever." (Isaiah 40:6-8). The best or worst of human relationships flower and fade with time. Now we are focussing on remembering the beauty of the "flower" instead of its transience. We are reminded that only our relationship with God has permanence though even it is subject to change. The strength that Isabelle and I are gaining from remembering the past is helping us to prepare to climb out of the canyon with a new appreciation for the fragility of life.

I made another mistake. I WORE A HAT THAT WAS TOO BIG FOR ME. Let me explain. I am a scientist. Scientists look for answers to questions. We are trained to state a problem, control what environment we can, collect data, analyze the data, draw conclusions, and if possible, generalize the results. This is based on the belief that there is meaning and order in our physical universe. If that is true, then life is a puzzle in which we search to abstract meaning from each experience. In pondering the significance of Hattie's suffering and death, I was sure that I could work all this into a pattern that would make sense in the light of our earlier experiences. If I could not, then this is a glitch and should not have been allowed. God goofed! This line of reasoning was a big mistake. It implied that if I was not able to work through this experience to make it meaningful, then God was either not all powerful or He was not good! If He lacks either of these attributes, He is not God.

I could identify with "Jacob" in his reasoning. "My way is hidden from the Lord and my judgment is passed over from my God." (Isaiah 40:27). God didn't seem to understand our situation. My wife and I worked together as a team. I needed her inspiration and encouragement. She needed my counsel. When her condition continued to worsen, she asked me why, in spite of all the people who were praying for her, did she not get better? I had to say quietly, "Honey, I don't know." I bowed my head. Why did Hattie suffer so? Some people who knew her well told her that because she had served God all those years she had a right to demand that He remove the suffering and heal her. She did ask but wouldn't demand anything of God. God didn't heal her. I couldn't understand. I guess my hat was too big!

As I continued to read through the fortieth chapter of Isaiah, I learned that "there is no searching of His understanding." (Isaiah 40:28). The prophet ask the rhetorical questions: "Who hath directed the spirit of the Lord, or being his counsellor hath taught Him? With whom did He counsel and who instructed Him, and taught Him in the path of judgment, and taught Him knowledge, and shewed to Him the way of understanding?" (Isaiah 40:13,14). Evidently, there are some things that are too big to fit into my head. If I could fully understand God and His ways, He would not be God because I would have circumscribed Him with a finite mind.

Then I read: "He giveth power to the faint; . . .young men shall utterly fall: but they that wait upon the Lord shall renew their strength . . . they shall walk and not faint." (Isaiah 40:29-31). Even though my hat had been too big, I found the solution in trusting God to help me walk quietly in faith when I couldn't see or understand.

The distraught people to whom this prophecy was first written formed an alliance. They encouraged each other to think that the situation was not as bad as it appeared. They manufactured new idols. "They helped everyone his neighbor; and everyone said to his brother, Be of good courage. So the carpenter encouraged the goldsmith and he that smooths with the hammer him that smote the anvil, saying, It is ready for the soldering: and he fastens it with nails, that it should not be moved." (Isaiah 41:6-7). As I pondered these words, I realized that I TOO HAD BEEN MANUFACTURING IDOLS.

The men referred to in these verses were making idols in hopes that they could control their own destiny. If they manufactured a god then he would be under their control. Of course, I had not made a "graven image", but I am afraid that I had dictated to God how things should be. I even quoted Jesus words, "And whatsoever you shall ask in my name, that will I do, that the Father may be glorified in the Son. If you shall ask anything in my name, I will do it." (John 14:13-14). I reasoned with God that if Hattie, who was paralyzed from the neck down, would suddenly be made physically well, think how much glory the "Father" would receive. I prayed earnestly, pacing the floor at night in my motel room and trying to persuade God to see it my way. I had a scenario developed in my mind. When Jesus came to the pool of Bethesda, He did not heal everyone. According to the record, He healed only one man — the worst case. Clearly Hattie's condition was approaching that level. Perhaps Jesus was waiting to produce a miracle that would surprise even the most skeptical doctors and thus get glory to His name. I prayed that He would hurry up and completely heal her physically. I even gave Him some latitude in how He could do it. I quoted more scripture to press my claim. Hattie died.

Michelle made a similar mistake. In her new-found joy of being a Christian she thought that she could force Andy to become a Christian. She prayed and begged God to "make it happen." She coddled and pampered Andy thinking that she could persuade him with kindness. One day her pastor unwisely remarked: "Michelle, you are pampering Andy into hell!" That did it. She then became obstinate and nagged him frequently — begging and pleading with him to become a Christian. She was doing everything that she knew to do and had taken her pastor's remark seriously, therefore God was obligated to change Andy. It didn't work. God would not be manipulated into forcing Andy to become a Christian against his own will.

We blush to remember that we were trying to make an idol out of God. An idol is a "god" that is captive to you. It must obey you. By it, theoretically, you can manipulate others and control your circumstances. In returning to the scene in our minds, we find that both of us were working in an idol factory. Our concept of God was just that — ours. We were in control and dictating to God what to do. Is that not what idol building is all about? An idol is a god that you have imagined and therefore you can control?

When we are faced by a frightening situation that threatens our way of life or maybe even our life itself, it is time to call on the supernatural. We can guarantee that supernatural powers will be perceived by us as friendly if we manufacture them. We fashion gods according to our desires (even worthy desires) or superstitions. We create gods after our own image. "If I were god and had supernatural powers, what would I do in this situation?" We fill in the blanks and then our imagination goes to work and supposes that god in doing just that. When it doesn't happen, it blows our faith.

Idols carry with them a quality of sensibility and thus an air of reality. As a scientist, I was nearly mesmerized into thinking that if something couldn't be captured in a test tube or described by a mathematical formula, then it wasn't real. I knew that the spiritual existed, but was too aware of the things that could be seen. I made most of my judgments on the basis of what could be measured. Hattie was alive as long as I could see her heart beat in the monitor and she could respond when I touched her arm. The only cure that I could imagine was a physical one. After her death, I was forced to rethink my position. The foundations had been shaken. Was there anything that could not be explained by evidence collected from the physical world? I was brought to my senses when I realized that a least some of the love that I have for my children cannot be explained on the basis of animal instincts. The spiritual realm really is important. Michelle also felt that she had the right to expect God to change Andy while Andy perceived it as a power struggle.

In the case of my stint in the idol factory, I learned that even though I had the right to pray and ask my heavenly Father to return Hattie to health, that He knew the total picture and would do what was best for all of us. I was disappointed that He had not seen it my way. There probably will be times again when I will feel deserted by nearly everyone, including God, but when my faith is revived, I will realize that God is still in control of my life as I have not withdrawn my basic commitment to Him. Michelle still has trouble trying to see how anything good can come out of this "mess." While she was working in the idol factory she also was wearing a hat that was too big for her.

We are feeling along with these people who were living through this prophecy. Cyrus was gaining power. "Who . . . gave the nations before him, and made him rule over kings? He gave them as dust to his sword, and as driven stubble to his bow." (Isaiah 41:2 See also 41:25 and 43:13). I realized another mistake some of us were making. We were guilty of DIGITAL THINKING IN AN ANALOG WORLD. In the world of computers, there are two types: digital which computes by turning internal switches on or off, and analog which computes by continuously varying voltages between certain limits. I was of the opinion that everything could be put into one of two categories: good or bad. From this Scripture I was reminded that there are some good things with bad side effects, and some bad things that work for the good of God's children.

I was of the opinion that Hattie's death was all bad. Then I was prompted to think that she is no longer suffering. When she was alive, she endured considerable pain. She forced herself to go to work when she had to "walk down the wall" with her hands in order not to fall down on the way to her desk. She despised her walker, using it only occasionally. She finally became so ill that she couldn't sit up more than thirty seconds. The last month that she was at home she needed someone to take care of her. She insisted that she would be all right, but my children took vacations and my neighbor helped when my children weren't here so that I could take care of my duties at the university. Now that is all over. I have the freedom to come and go as I please without worrying about her welfare.

I am more sensitive to the suffering of others. Some people have said that I am a better listener now. When one person talked to me about his divorce, he felt that I understood some of the feelings that he was experiencing. There is a bond of friendship between me and a man who lost his wife by death. He tells me that he has been helped by this manuscript. In addition, I have lost some of my self-sufficiency. Hattie and I worked as a team. It seemed that we could be completely independent. We never asked favors of anyone outside our immediate family. I vividly recall the first time that I needed to ask a friend to take me to the airport. When we arrived, I tried to pay him. He refused. I cried because I felt that I had to admit that I needed a friend. In other ways it is apparent that my frustration threshold is lower now. Not only am I aware of my diminished self-sufficiency but I am impatient when I am locked in a traffic jam or must wait in queue at the grocery store. Perhaps it is because I sense my mortality. I have so much to do and so little time to do it. My new sensitivity, my new dependency, my lower frustration trigger have some good aspects and bad aspects. I am beginning to adjust my thinking to fit the analog world we live in.

Another facet of this mistake is thinking about failure and success. I have a tendency to think of a project's outcome in terms of complete success or utter failure. Larry made this mistake too. However, he is finding some help in correcting this mistake. He has gone to a counselor who has helped Larry to see how some of the seemingly isolated events are contributing to the larger picture. The divorce is not entirely his fault nor is it entirely Cynthia's fault. The counselor has helped Larry to see that events in Cynthia's past contributed to her deciding to leave him.

As Cynthia was growing up, a traumatic incident occurred that left her feeling isolated from the rest of the family. She learned to be lonely even in a crowd. However, her father reached out to her and she felt accepted by him. The wholesome father-daughter relationship gave Cynthia some stability while her relationship with her mother remained strained. To assuage her pain, she sought comfort in alcohol and tobacco. Because of Larry's allergy, Cynthia gave up smoking when they started to contemplate marriage. After they married, she also gave up alcohol.

After they had been married for a few years, Cynthia gave birth to a little girl. The anticipation of this joyous event turned to horror when she was born badly deformed and lived only a few days. The baby died on May tenth. The pain of loneliness of her childhood now returned compounded with guilt and failure. "I can't even give Larry a healthy baby."

In Cynthia's opinion, Larry always succeeded. It seemed to Cynthia that he had everything together, while her growing feeling of failure gnawed at her sense of personal worth. So when Larry suggested that he might go to the university, she urged him to perhaps hoping that he would fail. When he succeeded at that too, the wedge was driven a little farther into their relationship. "Look at all that I have given up – and for what?"

For a number of years, Cynthia had had casual contact with her mother, but that "closeness" was missing. Then her mother developed lung cancer. The regimen of operations, radiation therapy and chemotherapy seemed to work. Cynthia showed concern for her mother but there was no clear reconciliation. Her mother went to visit a friend in another state. The disease returned and she was hospitalized. As soon as she was able to travel, Larry and Cynthia brought her back home. That night she stayed with them in the apartment. About two o'clock in the morning, she had a bad coughing spell. Larry went in to check on her and decided that Cynthia's mother was in deep trouble. They took her to the hospital. She was admitted. She died soon after — on May tenth!

The load of false guilt that Cynthia felt was increased by the loss of her mother on the same day; that is, May tenth, that Larry and Cynthia's baby died. This prolonged her "self-pity trip."

The counselor helped Larry to realize that the failure of his marriage was not a simple failure on his part. Cynthia's sense of failure (although she was really successful in her work and other areas of her life) was, in her mind, aggravated by living with Larry whom she perceived as always being successful. Her sense of guilt in other relationships eroded her relationship with Larry. When Larry couldn't afford to support her fantasies, Cynthia decided to move out. It was not a clear case of failure on Larry's part but had "analog" components.

Something that I am ashamed to confess is that I CARRIED A GOOD-LUCK CHARM in my head. "When you pass through the waters, I will be with you; and through the rivers, they shall not overflow you: when you walk through the fire, you shall not be burned; neither shall the flame kindle upon you." (Isaiah 43:2). This was a promise that everything would be as I envisioned it. It was incredible to me that anything bad could happen as long as I had this promise to lean on. If anything bad seemed to be threatening, then I would quote this Scripture and God would step in and protect me. When Hattie's cancer was diagnosed the first time, we wondered about this "charmed" life. Then cobalt radiation therapy seemed to cure the cancer. It seemed as though the charm was working. We even passed the magic five-year mark and began to breathe easy. Then at seven years it struck again. It was all down hill from there. What had happened to my promise? I discovered that I had read it "If . . ." and not "When . . ." The verse really says that we must pass through difficult situations. When that happens, we can be assured that God sets the limits.

I THOUGHT THAT I COULD SEE, BUT I WAS BLIND. My wishful thinking made me interpret circumstances unrealistically. Quoting the prophet: "They have not known nor understood: for he hath shut their eyes, that they cannot see; and their hearts, that they cannot understand. And none considers in his heart, neither is there knowledge nor understanding . . . He feeds on ashes: a deceived heart hath turned him aside, that he cannot deliver his soul, nor say, 'Is there not a lie in my right hand?'" (Isaiah 44:18-20) When Hattie began having black-out spells, I should have known that she was critically ill. In previous chapter (Chapter 7), I mentioned the one in Mobile. Also I mentioned in a previous chapter, (Chapter 3) that on another occasion, the doctor thought that Hattie ought to enter the local hospital. Everything seemed under control. The next time I was able to see her, she told me that they had had some excitement. When they took her blood pressure, it seemed o.k. Then, as the doctor had instructed, they asked her to stand to take another reading. Her blood pressure dropped to zero and she blacked out. They treated her symptomatically, giving her a blood protein to increase the volume of her blood. I should have understood then the seriousness of the matter, but I was blind. Her recovery was dramatic and that was all I needed.

There were times when Hattie would have intense pains at the base of her skull. To help, I tried to massage her shoulders and work my way up her neck. When that made the pain more intense, I stopped. I was frustrated, but never suspected that the pain indicated problems with her brain stem. She had leg cramps at night. She lost some control of body functions. She was nause-ated nearly every night. Even after she became paralyzed in the hospital, I was blind. One of the doctors tried to tell me that there was little hope. As time went on, he indicated that she would need to be on a respirator the rest of her life. I was angry because he tried to help me see. I was blind but didn't know it.

It has been very depressing to realize the mistakes we have made. They have been honest mistakes of the head and not of the heart. But there is also encouragement in these passages of scrip-ture. In spite of our blindness, God has not thrown us out. He inspired the prophet to write: "Hear, you deaf; and look, you blind, that you may see. Who is blind, but my servant? or deaf, as my messenger that I sent." (Isaiah 42:18-19) "Fear not: for I have redeemed you, I have called you by your name; you are mine." (Isaiah 43:1) .We are still His servants!

God speaks again: "I will bring the blind by a way that they knew not: I will lead them in paths that they have not known: I will make darkness light before them, and crooked things straight." (Isaiah 42:16). There is a future. There are still things to do. By acknowledging our mistakes we are better prepared to face this future with God. We are still experiencing frustrations and can't understand. In spite of God's promise, there are times of discouragement. There is the temptation to fall into our old ways of thinking and make the same mistakes over again. But God's presence is not to be measured by our mood or feelings. He has promised to be with us and His word is dependable.

Whew! That was tough for us. How about you? I am glad that we are this far along the road to the top.

CHAPTER 10

THE ART OF ASKING THE WRONG QUESTIONS

Summary: We ask questions for various reasons. Sometimes our questions are meaningless. Most of the time the "frame of reference" of the question is taken for granted, but if the questioner is in a different frame from the one answering, the answer is often bewildering. The disciples came into Jesus' frame of reference only after Pentecost. My frame of reference was corrected by the death of my late wife.

While we are resting after that brisk climb, look over there to the left. That slope is gradual and it looks easy. I wish we had someone to ask about it. What kind of questions would you like to ask?

"Does the trail provide for good solid footing?"

"Are there places to rest on the trail?"

"How far is it to the rim?"

While we wait here for a few minutes shall we consider the nature of questions. Why do we ask questions? What determines the nature of the questions that we ask? Allow me to philosophize a bit.

To ask questions seems to be part of our human nature. We

seek answers to satisfy our curiosity. For example, some children can ask questions that stump even the best minds. "Mommy, how can God see us here at home and daddy at work at the same time?" Or "Mommy, where is God's home?" To answer these sincerely to the satisfaction of a curious five-year-old is a challenge.

We ask questions in search of important information. When I was doing research in physics, I asked questions of nature about radiation damage to the DNA foundation molecules. Or when I was in Montgomery, Alabama for the first time to attend an important meeting, I had to stop and ask questions about how to get to the Madison Hotel. When I meet someone, I tell them my name in an implied question: "What is your name?"

We often ask questions when something happens that confuses us. We seek clarification. We think we have things figured out but want to make sure. We feel that God leading us in a certain path. We can anticipate "B", even predict "B" of the future. Then comes the "bend in the road." In our confusion, we ask questions.

Sometimes our questions are difficult to answer because of our limited understanding. I remember when I was teaching "Atomic and Nuclear Theory" to a class of eighth graders. I tried to reach the whole class. There was one fellow, however, that sat in the back of the classroom and looked bored. He acted as though he wasn't listening and what little he heard, he did not comprehend. After describing the size of the hydrogen nucleus compared to the size of the atom, I said, "So the hydrogen atom must be mostly empty space." My student's hand went up! I thought, finally I got through to him. He asked, "What is empty space?" This is a question that is either grasped intuitively or is the subject of philosophical debate. I was stumped. I mumbled something and went on. I felt that I had struck out.

Then sometimes our questions don't make any sense. For example: "How long is green?" or "When is Columbus, Ohio?" or even "Where is yesterday?" Other questions like: "How fast were you going?" can be correctly answered with several seemingly contradictory answers depending on the frame of reference. I remember sitting on a train in the station in Philadelphia, Pennsylvania on New Year's Eve. The blind was up and I could see another train within an arm's length from us. We were waiting for our train to change engines — from the smoky chug-chugging steam engines to the sleek purring diesels. Soon our train began to move without the usual jerking that occurs when the train changes engines. I commented, "That engineer really knows his stuff." We picked up speed and I was happy to be on my way to Boston finally. Only all too soon, the train next to us disappeared and I found that our train was still sitting in the station! If you had asked me before the other train disappeared if we were moving, I would gladly have testified in court that we were. It was all from the point of view – the frame of reference. So it is that sometimes the question is an inappropriate question because it comes from a misinterpretation of circumstances or misunderstanding of the purpose of the teacher. Even after three years of concentrated training, Jesus disciples did not understand His frame of reference.

Many years earlier, the prophets had predicted that a Messiah would come. For example: "For unto us a child is born, unto us a son is given: and the government shall be upon his shoulder: and his name shall be called Wonderful, Counsellor, The mighty God, The everlasting Father, The Prince of Peace. Of the increase of *his* government and peace there shall be no end, upon the throne of David, and upon his kingdom, to order it, and to establish it with judgment and with justice from henceforth even forever. The zeal of the Lord of hosts will perform this." (Isaiah 9:6-7).

But by the time Jesus appeared, the prophets had long been silent. There had been troubling times. Finally the Romans conquered the land and exacted heavy taxes. Peter and his friends felt the tax burden in their fishing business. But then Jesus became a popular teacher. One day He borrowed Peter's boat for a pulpit. In return, he enabled Peter to miraculously catch two boatloads of fish. Now, with Jesus, there was hope of relief from the political oppression and heavy taxation. Later, Jesus came by again and called Peter, his brother and his fisherman partners to follow him. They were excited to do so because they were becoming convinced that Jesus was the Messiah. So they followed Jesus. As they listened, Peter, Andrew, James and John became more and more convinced that they had made the right choice to follow Jesus. Day after day, they were impressed with the power of this man. He could feed a crowd with a lad's lunch, walk on the water, speak to the sea and it became calm, make the demon-possessed well, make the blind to see, make the lame to walk and even raise the dead. Was there anything that He could not do?

Sometimes our questions are evident from our statements. For example, Jesus and His apostles were on vacation. As they relaxed, conversation turned to the effectiveness of the message of Jesus. "What have you heard about who they think that I am?" Responses varied from the recently beheaded John the Baptizer to ancient Elijah and a list of other prophets. At least they recognized that Jesus spoke the voice of God. Then Jesus zeroed in on them – "What about you? Do you understand who I am?" Peter proudly replied for the group. With an air of certainty he boldly proclaimed: "You are the Christ of God." Peter's personal stock soared when Jesus commented him. "That is no ordinary insight. It could only have come to you from God Himself."

As they were returning from their vacation, Peter was feeling extra proud of his leadership. He was on Jesus' inner circle with his friends James and John. He had proclaimed his faith in Jesus mission and it had been affirmed. He was building dream-castles, envisioning his future in a kingdom that could not fail. But what is this that Jesus is saying? "I must go to Jerusalem and there the religious authorities will have Me beaten and finally killed." Peter couldn't stand it. So he gently took Jesus by the arm and led Him slightly away from the group to talk with Him in private. "Master, I hate to disagree with you, but what You are saying is all wrong. You see the Messiah is to be a kingly ruler to enforce His will on the nations of the earth. You are just depressed because our vacation is over." Jesus response was firm, sudden and sharp: "Get

away from Me, Satan! You are trying to trip me up! You are looking at My mission from a strictly human point of view." Peter was
crushed. He slinked back into the group and became very sullen.
He was utterly confused.

It was six full days later that Jesus said to Peter, James and
John, "Let's go mountain climbing." Peter was happy to be
welcomed back into the inner circle after his estrangement. Time
had lessened the sting of Jesus' rebuke and now it was time to be
healed completely. The climb up the mountain was invigorating.
When they reached the peak, the view was inspiring, but the thin
air made Peter, James and John drowsy and they dosed off.
Shortly they roused up becoming aware that as Jesus was praying,
His appearance was altered. They couldn't really describe it. His
body became nearly transparent and the inner glow of His personality shone through. Even His clothing glowed like a starched
shirt under black light. While the disciples watch in fascination,
two ethereal beings appeared. Soon it was obvious that it was two
men from the past. Peter whispered to John, "Do you suppose
that they are Moses and Elijah?" As the disciples listened, they
became sure that it was indeed Moses and Elijah. Jesus, Moses
and Elijah were in serious conversation about Jesus' coming
ordeal in Jerusalem. The ancients were strongly encouraging
Jesus to go through with the plan. Peter was nearly enchanted by
what he was experiencing. He even interrupted their conversation
with a suggestion. "Do you want me to gather some materials and
make three shelters up here? I would be glad to make one for you,
Jesus, and one each for your friends." It was as though Jesus
didn't hear him. Suddenly a bright cloud enshrouded the mountain top and blocked out their view in a heavy fog. A voice thun-
dered out of the cloud — really frightening but intelligible —
"This is My beloved Son, listen to Him!" The disciples huddled
on the ground in fear. When the cloud passed, they slowly looked
around. The only person that they saw was Jesus.

On the way down the mountain as they discussed the experience, Jesus further explained what He, Moses and Elijah were

talking about. As a matter of fact, it was the very thing that Peter had criticized Jesus for saying just a few days before. They asked, "What about the coming of Elijah?" Jesus said that Elijah had already come but was not recognized. He had been disposed of. (Matthew 16:13 — 17:13).

Throughout the whole episode, Peter was operating from a false notion of what it meant to be the Messiah. God was patiently trying to tell the disciples that they had the wrong perspective, but they were slow learners. In spite of God's instruction and Jesus' explicit details of what was about to happen, the question that lurked in the back of the disciple's minds was always the same: "Is it time yet? When will we be rich and powerful?" (Acts 1:6).

Some time later, Jesus was in Galilee and decided to head south toward Jerusalem. He had done that often before, but this time was different. The disciples noticed the change in Jesus' demeanor. He jaw was set. His eyes mirrored determination. His face was like a flint. His whole body language spoke of resolution. The twelve disciples who knew Him best were almost afraid. They hung back a little way and talked in hushed tones about what was about to happen. Maybe this is it. Maybe this is the "time." Of course, Jerusalem is the natural place for the initial confrontation and then from the "throne of David," the conflict will spread until the whole world will be under control of Jesus and his disciples.

On the way there, Jesus welcomes infants! His disciples tried to protect Him from these mothers. "Jesus is weighted down with serious business and you are bringing your infants for Him to hold? I don't think so!" But Jesus scolded the disciples and blessed the infants saying that they were the essence of the kingdom. Once again it is obvious that Jesus "frame of reference" was different from his disciples.

The disciples were not the only ones that were having difficulty in understanding "where Jesus was coming from." There was an influential young man who had been thrust into leadership. He attributed his good fortune to the fact that he was a good man, having kept the commandments from a very young age. There was something appealing about Jesus' ministry. This young ruler felt that something was lacking in his life. As soon as he could break free from his responsibilities for a short time, he rushed up to Jesus. After he had caught his breath, he asked Jesus, "Good Master, What must I do to inherit eternal life?" (Mark 10:17).This was apparently a wrong question. Why?

In the first place, the young man's focus of the word "good" was wrong. Goodness was associated with what one does. Matthew records the question: "What good thing must I do to inherit eternal life?" (Matthew 19:16). Jesus recognized this problem and tried to steer him to see things from another point of view. Earlier in His ministry, Jesus had been asked the same question. (Luke 10:25). Jesus responded with the question: "What do you understand that the law requires?" The man quoted *shema* and added "you shall love your neighbor as yourself." Jesus commended the lawyer and said, "If you do this, you shall live." However, this young man focused on the outward aspects of the law. "Don't steal, don't murder, don't commit adultery, don't bear false witness, honor your father and mother." He needed to focus on the goodness of God.

Another problem came as a natural misconception for a young man that was conversant in the covenantal law. The idea of doing something to obligate God to give him eternal life seemed to come naturally from his study of the Scriptures. Deuteronomy teaches that if you obey God's commands, you will be blessed. He no doubt thought that his wealth came as a result of obeying the commandments of God. He thought that eternal life would be his "inheritance" of he added another list of activities to his current list. However, Jesus had just told the crowd as he blessed the infants that the kingdom of heaven was made up of such as these. "Whoever does not receive the kingdom of God as a small child can not enter it." (Luke 18:17). From that frame of reference, eternal life is a gift. It is given to those who trust entirely in the grace of their Heavenly Father and not in doing something to earn it. Jesus corrected him as gently as He could but pointed out that he had to get rid of his wealth because it stood in the way of his trusting God. The man preferred his old frame of reference.

In spite of all these lessons and "object" lessons, the disciples did not come into Jesus' frame of reference. The kingdom of God was a political one and the disciples were on the inside track for positions of power and wealth. When the rich young ruler went away sorrowful, Peter called their sacrifices to the attention of Jesus. "What are we to receive for all that we have given up?" Jesus patiently answered them from His point of view. They still didn't get it. Then He tried to bring them into His frame of reference by predicting what was about to happen. "Behold, we are going up to Jerusalem, and everything which is written by the prophets about the Son of Man will be accomplished. For He will be delivered to the Gentiles, and will be mocked and abused and spit upon, and after they have scourged Him, they will kill Him; and the third day He will rise again." (Luke 18:31-33). They still didn't get it even though He had been explicit.

Peter has been speaking for the "twelve" but now John's and James' mother puts in a request. "Lord, when you come into your kingdom may my sons sit one on your right and the other on your left?" It is obvious that they did not have a clue what they were asking. The competition for positions of power were in line with their mindset. They were still were thinking that the climax of Jesus ministry would be the overthrow of the Romans and the conquest of the entire world. Being on the right hand and on the left implied positions of prestige and power. Jesus asked them a question to try to set them straight: "Are you able to pay the price that I am about to pay?" They answered in bold ignorance, "Most certainly!" Then Jesus said that the positions that they requested had been assigned but they would indeed suffer like He would suffer — rejection, persecution, misunderstanding including physical and emotional pain. The other disciples were enraged that James and John had gotten first dibs.

The excitement mounts as they approach Jerusalem. Jesus asked two of the disciples to go into the village and borrow a colt. When they returned, they put their cloaks on the colt and Jesus mounted. The emotional tide rose, being contagious, until the whole crowd was shouting, "Hosanna to the king." Jesus didn't stop them. The disciples were caught up in the moment and felt like their sacrifices were paying off; their questions were being answered; their expectations were being realized and their confidence was being justified. They were ready to predict the play by play from here. Jesus riding into Jerusalem as proclaimed king would be confronted by the authorities and by His supernatural power would blast them from their positions and He would "sit on the throne of David." The true sons of Israel would rally around Him. The conflict would spread until the Roman officials would mobilize forces against Him. But He would outwit them, easily winning a military victory. He would be proclaimed ruler of the world and there would be lasting world peace. Since the twelve had been His inner circle and had stuck with Him when others were leaving, they would soon be powerful and rich.

Right on schedule, Jesus cleansed the temple. As expected, that aroused the temple authorities. By shear force, He drove out the cattle, sheep and the "money-changers." As they were leaving, Jesus was heard to be lamenting — "Oh Jerusalem, Jerusalem, you who kill the prophets and messengers that are sent to you. How I would like to protect you as a mother hen protects her chicks, but you stubbornly refused. Your house is now left unto you — desolate." (Matthew 23:37ff) The disciples were again perplexed. They called Jesus' attention to the beauty of the temple. They noted the large stones in the foundation of the courtyard. They pointed out the sturdy architecture. Jesus was unimpressed. His response further confused them. "You see all these things that you are pointing out. They will be completely destroyed. The stones that make up the temple will be scattered."

This prompted another question: "When will this happen? What will be the signs of your coming as king and the end of the age?" Actually the disciples asked three questions but they thought that they were all the same question. From their point of view, the destruction of the temple (and its rebuilding) would coincide with the proclamation of Jesus as king and that would be the end of the present age. An age for peace in a new dimension would be ushered in and with it a new way of life. The inevitable "when" question had surfaced again. Jesus' answer confused them. He, from our perspective of the centuries, was talking of His Second Coming. They had no conception of His "second" coming. He was here now and would set up an earthly kingdom. The clincher came with His statement: "There will be an end of the age, but no one knows when it will be — not any man; not any angel; not even I. You see, the Father alone is the One to decide that." (Matthew 24:36).

Jesus tries again to help them into His frame of reference. Prior to the "Last Supper," Jesus performs the lowly servant's task — or the task of the youngest child, if the family didn't have servants — of washing the apostle's feet. They were embarrassed and ashamed but still "didn't get it!" Jesus spelled out the rules of the kingdom. The greatest will be the one who performs the lowest tasks. "I am among you as one that serves."

At the conclusion of the meal, Jesus talked seriously about His imminent departure. The disciples asked, "Can we go with You?" Jesus said that He had to go alone. Peter asked, "Why can't I go? I am willing to die in Your defense!" Jesus sadly responded, "Really? Before morning you will strongly deny that you have any connection with Me or that you even know Me." The disciples were thinking in terms of political power, of an earthly kingdom and of personal prestige and wealth.

The mock trials came. The crucifixion quickly followed. The disciples' dreams were shattered. Confusion was the order of the day. Fear of being identified with "the late" Jesus kept them pretty much in hiding. "How could we have been so wrong?" They tried to sort through the ashes of their dreams. "What could be salvaged from the experience of the last three years?" Then into their confused minds came the voices of women nearly hysterical with joy — "Jesus is alive! He rose from the dead! He is no longer in the tomb but has risen 'like He said!'" Then Jesus materialized in the room that had been carefully secured. Mind overload! It must be a ghost or hallucination, but all of those present saw Him. He spoke with a firm, authoritative voice. He ate real physical food. He invited anyone who wanted to the feel his hands and feet.

On later occasions, Jesus appeared and talked with large crowds (five hundred at once) or small (individuals such as Peter). The confusion was beginning to clear. The crucifixion was apparently a brief detour. Peter was forgiven and restored to a position of leadership. Then as the disciples were assembled on the Mount of Olives, Jesus was giving them some instructions. The old question came up again: "Is it time yet? Are You going to make it happen? Now are we going to displace the Romans and be powerful and rich?" Jesus answer confused them again because they were still operating from their old frame of reference. Jesus patiently replied, "It is not for you to know the times or the seasons which the Father has reserved for Himself to determine, but, yes, you will receive power! Not political power, but power to witness starting at home and spreading the good news through the entire earth. Wait in Jerusalem until this power comes." (Acts 1:6-8). When it finally came on the Day of Pentecost, they finally moved into God's frame of reference and the story of the changes is recorded in the Acts of the Apostles.

God has often made changes in my frame of reference. Because of the continual bombardment by the every-present physical environment, my frame of reference becomes warped. The most serious warp came when my late wife, Hattie, lay paralyzed in the CCU unit of a hospital in Birmingham, Alabama. One of the interns kept insisting that Hattie could not recover. I couldn't buy that. I knew that God could bring physical healing and restore her to perfect health. I visualized many more years of family happiness on this earth. When the chief doctor who had always been optimistic said, "I am afraid that we are losing this battle." I was shocked into God's frame of reference. "I have prayed for her healing. Maybe that is God's way of healing her permanently." The doctor hesitated and then quietly responded: "Maybe so." Through the painful days that followed her death, I was sustained by the faith that God had healed her by promoting her to her permanent heavenly home where she enjoys perfect health today. "Forgive me. I guess I got carried away."

Isabelle, who has been sitting quietly, speaks up: "I have been wondering why everyone seems to be picking on me! 'Why do other people get all the breaks?' So much so that I even dream about it. The other night I dreamed that I was near a large house with a big porch. I walked up onto the porch by holding onto the handrail. I staggered to the window and looked in. There were all kinds of 'goodies' on the table and the people in the room were enjoying the food and friendship. I was nearly famished while others were feasting. I tapped on the window but there was no response. I crawled to the front door but was too weak to open it. I woke up hungry and discouraged. I asked, 'Why me?' I was in the depths of a 'pity party.'

"Then I prayed, asking the Lord these questions. He helped me to see His hand at work in my life. I have always loved both the beach and the mountains. He led me to a place that they are both within easy driving distance. He helped me to be aware of the love that my family, though distant in miles, has for me. He assured me of His love and care for me. I was drawn into a closer relationship with Him. In this frame of reference I am aware that I was focusing on the wrong things, asking the wrong questions."

Jim and Susie were whispering thoughtfully and then Jim confesses: "Susie and I have been asking 'Why us?' Arthur's illness has put a strain on our budget. The emotional pain that we feel is nearly unbearable. Now we are considering the worldwide problem of evil and the incidence of debilitating disease. In this new frame of reference, the question becomes: 'Why not us?' Children with special needs need special parents. Although we don't feel like special parents, we trust that God knows what He is doing."

Oh, here is someone now. "Sir, could you tell us about the trail to the left there? Is it as smooth and safe as it looks? And how far is it to the rim of the canyon?"

"You are asking the wrong questions because you are looking in the wrong direction. That trail is relatively smooth, has a gentle slope. It would be a good trail to take if you just wanted to take a walk. But out of your sight it ends in a blind canyon with vertical walls and no hand or toe holds. If you traveled that trail you would have to return here and take another trail if you want to reach the mesa. Look to the right. In spite of the difficulty of this trail, it will lead you to the mesa again."

"Thank you!"

CHAPTER 11

THROWN DOWN BUT NOT DESTROYED

Summary: Most of us have been perplexed, lonely, and/or discouraged at some time in our life. The Apostle Paul learned to cope with these problems by being aware of his "earthen vessel" and the great treasure that it contained.

"Whew! That man was not joking when he said that this is a difficult trail. I think that I am going to need some help."

"Well, don't you have your Bible? Couldn't we find something there to help us?"

"Who had trouble in the Bible and yet came out on top?"

"How about the Apostle Paul?"

"Good choice! Why don't we review some of the things that he experienced?" He had spent quite some time in various prisons. Five times his own countrymen had beaten him to nearly the limit of the law. Three times the Romans had ordered him beaten with rods. Once he was stoned with real stones and left for dead. Three times he had been shipwrecked. One of those times he was adrift for about 24 hours before he was rescued. In addition to that, he had been accosted by highway robbers, threatened by heathen and religious people alike and especially abused by those who claimed to be Christians but were really hypocrites. He had exercised himself in religious disciplines, had been cold, had been tired and had been hungry. (2 Corinthians 11:24-27). In addition to all this, he had some kind of physical ailment that he called a "thorn in the flesh" (2 Corinthians 12:7) that impaired his effectiveness as an evangelist.

Look. Here is a statement about how he was afflicted (KJV says "troubled on every side" 2 Corinthians 4:8). I think that we can agree with him, at least on that score.

Sarah admits feeling afflicted until I read the list of the Apostle Paul's afflictions. For her, everything was normal until her husband died. Then her world fell apart. He had been the "head of the house" in a good sense. She had relied on him to make the major decisions. He was stable and consistent — always there to help. When he died, an important part of her was gone. Although Mike is "a good boy," he is a teenager. He is easygoing and not serious about anything. His schoolwork doesn't seem important to him. Then Sarah recently lost her job without warning because she was not given proper instruction when she was hired. All this added up to her feeling "afflicted" until she got to thinking about Paul.

Similarly, Isabelle is feeling afflicted. I don't need to recite again all of her troubles. In addition to her mother's death, being lied to about her job, being frustrated in trying to help her youthful charges, she is bothered by her friends who ridicule her for her Christian moral standards. Her afflictions are the cause of much emotional pain.

Did Paul bring this on himself? In some ways he did. When he became a Christian, it angered some of his old friends until they wanted to kill him. Some of his new friends helped him escape from the city "through a window in a basket . . . down by the wall." (2 Corinthians 11:23). He returned to Jerusalem only to cause a disturbance there by boldly preaching the gospel. When a group planned to kill him, once again his Christian friends spirited him away, helping him escape to this home town. (Acts 9:29-30).

Later, Barnabas looked him up and asked him to help in the work of the church at Antioch. Then he and Barnabas started to travel around the Roman Empire, preaching the Gospel.

On the next trip, Barnabas took his nephew and went one way while Paul and Silas went another. By a vision, Paul was invited to Europe to help the Macedonians. He and his companions came to Philippi. There they were welcomed into a prayer group. With the support of this group, they were trying to develop a congregation, but they had some unwanted advertising. A slave girl, with some uncanny ability to "tell fortunes" kept following them around and announcing loudly, "These men are servants of the most high God which show us the way of salvation." (Acts 16:17). Paul became annoyed by this and turned to the girl and commanded her "spirit of divination" to depart from her. She became sane that same moment and her slave-masters were very angry. They dragged Paul and Silas into court and accused them of teaching "customs which are not lawful for us to receive, neither to observe, being Romans." (Acts 16:21). This, of course, was not true, because Paul was a Roman citizen and proud of it. However, the magistrate did not bother to investigate the charges. Paul and Silas were stripped, flogged, and jailed. That night, Paul couldn't sleep because of his sore back. About midnight, he whispered, "Silas, are you asleep?" Silas responded, "Are you kidding?" They began to converse about the cause of the mess they were in. To some people it may seem strange, but the conversation excited them. In spite of tired, sore bodies, they were happy in spirit. They began to praise, pray and sing. The earth shook, the doors of the prison flew open and their stocks were unlocked. When the jailer woke and saw what had happened, he was about to commit suicide. Paul assured him that no one had escaped. Paul then told him about Christ and as a result, the jailer and his family became Christians. The next day, the magistrates ordered their release, but Paul used his Roman citizenship to force the magistrates to lead a parade through the streets to indicate that Paul and Silas were not criminals as they had been accused.

Notice, though, Paul wrote, we are "afflicted but not made to quit." Even after assessing all these afflictions, Paul was not ready to give up his Christianity nor his ministry. I guess we need to hang in there.

Perhaps you can identify with the writer when he says, "We are perplexed . . . ." He was perplexed about the manner in which some people subscribed to ideas that were contradictory to or actions that were inconsistent with their Christian profession. (2 Corinthians 15; and Galatians 3). With respect to some of the difficult theological problems that he considered, he concluded: "O the depths of both the wisdom and knowledge of God! How unsearchable are His judgments and His ways past finding out!" (Romans 11:33). There was a period when he puzzled about his "thorn in the flesh" and why God did not remove it.

That resonates with me. I am trained to asked questions about things in my environment. As a scientist, my search for truth is based on the belief that there is a rational order to this physical universe. This attitude carries over into my personal life. Since Hattie's death, it seems that there is a plethora of unanswered questions about things that really matter. One of the big questions is: "Why are some people delivered from death and others delivered by death?" Also one does not need to look very far to detect much cruelty in nature. Then the problem of suffering and death among small, innocent children raises its head. You probably know some people that cheat, lie, and steal who seem to prosper more than others who are scrupulously honest. There are those who have habits that have been proven deleterious to one's health and yet are more healthy than others who are careful to follow all the health rules. Indeed, I am perplexed.

Suppose we assume a chaotic universe, that there is no God, and that the fundamental force in the universe is impersonal. Love is an illusion. Blind fate controls our circumstances. This might solve the problem of perplexity, but it introduces a much worse one: despair. Despair drives people insane. It makes one quit trying. It is the dead end of the road with the return trip blocked. It is surrender to the worst imaginable, making it seem inevitable. It cannot coexist with hope. One thing that makes hell such a horrible prospect is that it is a place of hopelessness and despair.

Oh! Here is another thing that we have experienced: persecution, — well, "sort of." Michelle reacts: "This is my story. Life was tolerable before I became a Christian. Andy wanted to control me and I let him. He was 'Mr. Big,' ruling the family with an iron fist. After I became a Christian, I had a new 'Lord.' Jesus was the master of my life and Andy became so angry that he was ingenious in making things miserable for me and the children. I remember the day that our oldest son had done something to make Andy mad. He shook him vigorously. The boy said something and Andy grabbed him by the throat and threatened to kill him. I stepped in and shoved my son away from his daddy. Andy drew back his fist to hit me and I stood just stood there facing him. He got control of himself before he hit me. Andy knew that before I was a Christian I would not have interfered in his 'disciplining of the children.' (Actually, it was child abuse.) After that he found subtle ways of making me miserable. He attacked my self-esteem. He called my friends hypocrites. He accused me of having an affair with the preacher. He ridiculed me and the children for our 'goody-goody' way of life. If we ever did anything wrong, he would pounce on it with the remark: 'I thought you were a Christian!' He would quote and misquote Scripture and laugh because we did not know enough to point out his errors. Although he threatened violence, he never hit me and after the incident mentioned above, he was more reasonable with his treatment of the children. He did everything that he could think of to drive a wedge between me and my Lord. But I stuck with my Lord Jesus and He did not forsake me. So Andy 'kicked me out' and I am trying to figure out where I go from here." The group is sympathetic with Michelle. We are trying to encourage her.

In continuing the discussion, we ask: "What makes persecution so dreadful?" The constant battering of the psychological attacks by those who are supposed to be supporting us produces emotional pain. As in Michelle's case, there is no escape except a few hours a week when she and the children attend church. Sometimes physical pain is experienced. At other times persecution shows itself as public ridicule and the ostracism that is usually associated with it. In that sense, it is a lonely experience. You may be in a crowd, but lonely in your separation from it. You may not be persecuted as such, but perhaps you feel left out of everything that is important. At times I have. After it became known that Hattie had cancer, we experienced a considerable amount of rejection. One time at a "fellowship" meeting after church on Sunday evening, Hattie and I started to sit at a table with someone that we thought was our friend. She said, "Oh, This table is reserved." Of course we could have been invited to pull up a couple of extra chairs, but it was obvious to us that we were not welcome and so we left. At that point we were feeling very rejected. Later the person apologized.

If we are aware that someone in this world really cares about what happens to us, the "persecution" is easier to take. Paul relates the following incident. "Alexander the coppersmith did me much evil . . . for he has greatly withstood our words. At my first answer no man stood with me, but all forsook me . . . notwithstanding the Lord stood with me and strengthened me . . . and I was delivered out of the mouth of the lion." (2 Timothy 4:14-17). Persecution and loneliness will come, but it is made bearable by the knowledge of God's love.

On this trail we have tripped and it seems like we have been "cast down." Look, Paul admits that he was cast down by the actions of the Corinthians. The church was split into several groups, each promoting their favorite preacher or special piety. There was immorality that even the pagans would not condone. There were incidents of gluttony in the presence of hungry people at the church social functions. A segment of the church denigrated Paul's ministry because of his physical handicaps. These are a few things that threw Paul down but he would not be devastated by them.

When Hattie died, I felt as though I had been thrown down from the pinnacle of faith. I had preached about the joy of salvation, about the power of prayer, about faith that produced results, and about the reality of the unseen. By her death, my faith was shot down over enemy territory. For a time, I wondered if I could survive. I was knocked down. But God was patient with me and did not forsake me. Whenever the enemy of my faith was about to take me captive, I would get an invitation to preach and thus had to review the facts that had led me to believe in the first place. Over the past two years, God has helped restore my faith, heal my broken heart, and challenge me greater service than ever before.

My daughter, Julia, in spite of her own sorrow, has helped me immeasurably to think objectively. "Mother had to die sometime and we sure would not have wanted to lose you both at the same time." "Mother suffered considerable, as you well know. Now that is all over." " Mother would not have wanted to remain with us as an invalid. She was always so active. Besides that, she loved you too much to want to be a hindrance to you." My other children have supported me with their love and help me to know that I now have a doubly important role to play in their lives. All this love and emotional support helps me to sense that this transient life is only a phase of something much bigger that continues beyond the seen.

What was Paul's secret that kept him going when afflicted, that fought off despair when perplexed, that gave him a sense of God's presence when persecuted, and that helped him survive being thrown down? If we discover that, perhaps we can use the same techniques. "Look here. It talks about a treasure in earthen vessels." Good! Evidently the recognition of his humanity as an "earthen vessel" helped him keep his perspective.

There are several aspects of this "earthen vessel". It includes our physical body. Not all of us are equally endowed with health. If we lose our perspective then physical affliction may overwhelm us. If our "treasure" depends on feeling, a migraine headache may help us decide that we have lost it because we aren't effervescent. That, in turn, may lead us to conclude that we never did have a treasure. Jim speaks up: "Arthur's spirit is beautiful even though his 'earthen vessel' is badly deformed."

The "earthen vessel" includes our emotional make-up. Some people are more volatile by nature than others. Some people are more aggressive than others. Some people have a better sense of humor than others. Some people are more activity-oriented than others. If we don't recognize that each of us has a different emotional make-up, we open ourselves to hurt when someone doesn't act like we think a Christian should. On the other hand, we may excoriate ourselves because we do not seem to be as "Christian" as one of our acquaintances. Isabelle had problems because the emotional stress caused a breakdown in her body chemistry. She has had to learn about her "earthen vessel."

The "earthen vessel" includes our intellectual make-up. Some people grasp the meaning of a situation more quickly than others. Some people naturally have a deeper insight into what they read than others. Some people's minds are better organized than others. If we don't recognize our intellectual limitations, we may lose our faith when confronted with a problem that seems to have no rational solution. Andy took advantage of his superior intellect to belittle and ridicule Michelle because of her "earthen vessel."

Paul was aware of his limitations. He did not lose his faith just because he was stoned and left for dead and Barnabas wasn't. The next day he and Barnabas left town together to preach in another city. (Acts 14:20). Paul's prejudice against John Mark blinded him to the young man's value as a minister. (Acts 15:39). Later Paul acknowledged that he had been wrong. (2 Timothy 4:11). When Paul faced fierce opposition by those who claimed to be super-apostles, he was tempted to reveal some aspects of his "near-death" experience as proof that he was more spiritual than they. This pride would have led to sin. His "thorn in the flesh" kept him from that by reminding him that his treasure was in an "earthen vessel".

The nature of the treasure gave a historical perspective to his faith. Paul was trained in the Jewish law and tradition. To him, religion must have its roots in history. He was glad that he could trace his genealogy back to Abraham through Benjamin. (Philippians 3:5). He was a monotheist. He slavishly worshiped his God. Then one day, as he traveled to Damascus, a bright light knocked him to the ground. A voice said to him, "Saul, Saul, why do you persecute me?" Confused, Paul (i.e. also called Saul) asked who had knocked him down. The voice answered, "I am Jesus whom you are persecuting." Paul was then given instructions to follow. When the incident was over, Paul was blind.

He was led into the city and took lodging. For three days he fasted and prayed. Then a Christian man named Ananias came and prayed with him and Paul received his sight. It was good to see the light again, but even when blind, a light was beginning to shine in his heart. He recalled the biblical account of creation when order was brought out of chaos by the command of God: "Let there be light!" (Genesis 1:3). The light that shined at creation was dawning in his heart. "For God, Who commanded light to shine out of darkness, has shined in our hearts, to give the light of the knowledge of the glory of God in the face of Jesus Christ." (2 Corinthians 4:6).

It appears that Paul's inner life had been in chaos since his approving of the stoning of Stephen. His feverish activity in persecuting the church was fueled by his confusion. What Stephen had said before he was killed and the way he had died left Paul's soul unsettled. Now at last life was beginning to have meaning again.

Why don't you check your background as we recite some of ours? In the light of my perplexities and loneliness, I was forced to think back to my childhood when as a child I responded to the preaching of my father and "went forward" because of a burden of sin. I prayed and cried before God, asking Him to forgive me. A great sense of peace came into my young life at that point. I remember it clearly. The experience was real. I cannot deny it.

In my preteen years, I remember my spiritual pride. I was the pastor's son. I considered myself to be spiritually better than anyone I knew, especially other young people. One day Jesus told a story that described my situation. It was about a man who was a merchant. His specialty was pearls. He traveled around the country trying to find pearls that would be of interest to his customers. One day he came across a "Pearl of great price". After he had seen that gem, nothing else mattered until he possessed it for himself. After bargaining to get the best price, he figured his assets. Figuring every way he could, the result was always the same. In order to own that pearl he must sacrifice everything else. The drawing power of that great gem was so great that "he sold all that he had and bought it." (Matthew 13:45-46). I was searching for something to give value to your life. I came to believe that my pride was the major barrier to my obtaining this treasure. I had to surrender everything, including my pride, to Jesus. It was in an evangelistic meeting, once again I "went forward" in public acknowledgment of my desire for the "Pearl of great price." At that time, I made a commitment to God that all that I was or ever would be and all that I have or ever would have was now and forever dedicated to Him. There resulted a keen consciousness of the reality of God and that He had accepted my gift. A very strong sense of well-being came as a result. This to me was the "Pearl of great price."

When my father died about my twentieth birthday, I sensed that God was in control of the situation. Although I wept openly at his funeral and experienced a real sense of loss, there was still a deep realization that dad continued to live in a new dimension. Remembering these times helps to restore my faith in the gospel that I preach.

Sarah's father was born in a formal religious family. He had good moral values. When he was seventeen, he emigrated to the United States of America where he found work as a farmer. In a few years, he had saved some money and bought a farm. He was devout but his church attendance was irregular. After he married, he became more regular in church. He and his wife "raised Sarah in church." When Sarah was in her teens, she learned the "Way of Salvation"(2. Endnote) and started her own personal journey with Christ. This "treasure" kept her steady through many trying times. Now, she is drawing on her faith for strength and hope as she encourages us on our journey out of the canyon.

Isabelle's parents were Christians who lived their faith. She watched their consistent manner of life through the good times and the bad. After she started to public school and observed other families, she decided that she wanted the faith that kept her parents steady when the "going was rough." Talking to her mother, she learned the secret was a personal relationship with Jesus. She accepted Him as Lord of her life. She now says, "I would no doubt have committed suicide if it had not been for this 'treasure' in my 'earthen vessel.' God, through His Son Jesus, is my personal Friend."

Michelle was raised in a dysfunctional family. Her father had an alcohol problem and would become violent when he was drunk. Her mother was a hard-working, patient person that attended church when she could. The story of her conversion has already been told. (Chapter 6). Although she is in the canyon because of her faith, she testifies, "In spite of the uncertainty of the future, I am confident that God has a plan for my life."

In reading about Paul's "Damascus Road" experience, we understand that the light was not an impersonal bolt of lightning. Nor did Paul suffer from a sunstroke. Paul refers to this experience as imparting "knowledge of the glory of God in the face of Jesus Christ." A glimpse of the glory of God and things of this world become less significant. It is true that Paul knew how to enjoy a good meal and other material things when he had them. (Philippians 4:12). After his Damascus road experience, however, these were not given top priority. As a consequence, he could be afflicted and not give up and quit. He could be perplexed and not allow despair to control his life. He could be persecuted and not feel forsaken. He could be thrown down from his mountain-top experience and not be destroyed on the rocks of despair and doubt.

Once Paul had seen the glory of God in the face of Jesus Christ, he was able to keep going when things were rough. When he met Christ on the Damascus road, Paul was given a vision of the things that he was responsible for. It was difficult for him to understand. As life unfolded, he understood more and more that God would furnish the grace if he would furnish the person. It became evident that what he accomplished was possible because of a power beyond himself. The earthen vessel glowed with a power that transcended itself.

Some of my closest friends who know how much I loved Hattie have wondered how I can keep on working and preaching. I wish to testify with Paul: "We have this treasure in earthen vessels, that the excellency of the power may be of God and not of us." (2 Corinthians 4:7).

"That was a refreshing experience, wasn't it? Hey folks, doesn't that help us to have the energy to keep going?"

CHAPTER 12

DAILY GRACE

Summary: *If you are experiencing difficult circumstances at this time, consider Jesus' teaching on successful living. He taught and showed us how to live one day at a time, to minimize our worrying by ordering our priorities, and then letting God develop us naturally.*

Please let me share with you a couple of years out of my past when the Sermon on the Mount helped me survive and eventually climb out of a different canyon. Maybe we can both get help as I remember that experience.

"What will we have for supper?" seems like an innocent question, but there was a time when that question was inappropriate. I had just graduated from seminary, refused a hundred-dollar-a-week job to take a pastorate that promised to pay twenty five dollars a week. When we arrived at the parsonage we found a six-room, two-story house that was in poor condition. The kitchen was so filthy that the good people of the church suggested that we close it off and not use it. Two of the bedrooms were in need of repair. It didn't matter much, though, because we didn't have any furniture. Hattie was pregnant, which was not part of our original plan. When the finance company found that we had moved out of state, they wanted the $475 that we owed on the car immediately or they would repossess it. Neither Hattie's parents nor my mother had any reserve money to loan us. The bank would not loan us the money because they had the church's account and knew the financial status of the church. In a few weeks it became obvious that there would be some weeks that we would receive no salary so that the payment on the parsonage could be met. About this time that question was not, "What will we have for supper?," but "Honey, how do you want your potatoes cooked tonight?" (Thank God for potatoes!) I will confess that there were times I had trouble with the Scripture: "I have not seen the righteous forsaken, nor his seed begging bread." (Psalm 37:25) I felt forsaken!

Sarah wants to add her story. "My husband and I were living on a farm which I had inherited and he was preaching at a small church. Life was not rosy, but things were not bad. Then my husband received a call to a church about two hundred miles away. We felt that God was 'telling' us to go. So we left the farm and moved to 'the country!' It was a rural church located back in the hills. The parsonage was a mile from the church. The nearest town was over two miles away where there was a general store, a vocational school, a post office and a funeral home. Most of our parishioners lived within a fifteen-mile radius of the church. They eked out an existence and invited us to join them. We were supposed to be full-time pastors, but it took miracle after miracle to manage on the small salary that we received.

"I remember that my clothes were getting threadbare. I thought I needed a new dress. So I prayed. A couple of weeks later, one of the poorest members of the church came up to me. She handed me a bag and said, 'The Lord told me to give this to you.' I looked and it was a piece of material for a dress. I later found out that she had scraped and saved to buy the material to make a dress for herself. I felt bad. I cried. I had deprived this poor saint of God a dress. I asked God to forgive me.

"My father lived with us. He was in his nineties. One winter he got the flu that led to pneumonia. He died. It took all our savings and what we could scrape together to bury him. There was no money for Christmas presents for our ten-year-old son. (That was before Mike was born.) We were concerned. Would our son grow to resent the ministry because of this deprivation? Also, there was no food nor money for food for the next month. Early one cold morning we thought that we heard a car drive off. Upon investigating, we found a couple of bags on our porch. In it was a gift-wrapped wind-up tractor for our son and groceries to tide us over until we could buy some. God continued to provide for our needs plus a little extra for our son.

"Our house was heated by a potbelly, coal-burning stove. We also needed coal for our cook stove. The mine, about five miles away, allowed us to go to the slag pile and pick up what we called 'bony' which was slate with some coal mixed in with it. We would take burlap bags and load them up with this fuel. It took a lot of kindling to get it started, but once it caught, it made a hot fire. The 'ashes' were actually big cinders that had to be removed periodically. Things were not easy, but they weren't easy for our parishioners either. They shared with us and we shared with them. God blessed our community. I don't want to go back, but looking back, it was a time of spiritual blessing. We learned the truth that if we seek first God's kingdom and His righteousness, all these things (food, clothing, shelter) will be added to us."

"Thank you for sharing that with us and reminding us of the Scriptural promise. So let us look together at the Sermon on the Mount and to Jesus who had delivered it." He lived in a time of trouble. His life and ministry were in a small country that felt the economic pressure of supporting a foreign government. Nearly everywhere one went, he would find Roman soldiers or tax collectors. There seems to be a high probability that Joseph had died before Jesus started His ministry, leaving Jesus with the pressure of responsibility for His mother's welfare. He also felt the awesome responsibility of showing the world the true nature of God. How did He survive without going crazy?

He gives us a clue in His sermon: live one day at a time!

"Don't worry about tomorrow. Let tomorrow worry about itself. It can furnish enough problems without your help." (Matthew 6:34). I interpreted this as saying that <u>attitude</u> toward the problems of life is the key to survival.

I asked myself: "What is the best attitude to take toward food and drink?" Certainly Jesus would not expect us to starve ourselves. He taught His disciples to pray: ". . . Give us this day our daily bread. . . ." (Matthew 6:11). That seemed to indicate that God was interested in my finding nourishment to take care of my and my wife's bodies.

He did not scold his disciples for making provision for future meals. On at least two occasions, He taught a very large crowd until it was past time for them to eat. He then fed them a nutritious meal until everyone was satisfied. The disciples were then instructed to collect the "left-overs." In one case they filled twelve lunch-baskets, in the other case seven hampers. Why do you save "left-overs?" So they can be eaten another day. I came to believe that those of you who can raise a garden (I never could make things grow and produce!) and preserve the produce are in divine order.

He did not expect His disciples to hide in a corner and gobble their food in shame. It seemed perfectly proper to enjoy food and drink on a festive occasion. For example, consider the time that He was invited to a wedding feast. While Jesus and His disciples were there, the host ran out of wine. To add to the festivities, Jesus furnished plenty of the finest wine, made from water. This seems to be an endorsement of this kind of occasion. He also regularly participated in religious festivals. He enjoyed eating so much that He was accused by some of being a "gluttonous man." (Luke 7:34)

However, in the Scripture lesson Jesus said, "Take no thought for your life, what you shall eat or what you shall drink . . ." (Matthew 6:25). He also talked about clothing in the same passage, yet His only possession that seemed to be worth gambling over was His seamless robe!

How could I reconcile the apparent differences between what He taught and what He did? From the context of what He said, it appeared to me that He meant that food, drink, and clothing were not to be my primary concern in life. "Is not the life more than meat and the body more than raiment?" (Matthew 6:25) His perspective became more obvious to me as I examined a couple more incidents in His life.

At the beginning of His ministry, Jesus went into the desert to clarify His vision of His assignment. After forty days without anything to eat, He was naturally hungry. Even the stones began to remind Him of the bread His mother baked. Satan suggested that He indulge Himself by turning the stones to bread. He rebuked His Adversary by saying, "Man shall not live by bread alone, but by every word that proceeds out of the mouth of God." (Matthew 4:4) He was getting His priorities straight. Food is good, but it is not all important.

Another time, Jesus was traveling through Samaria. He rested by Jacob's well while His disciples went into town to get some food. While they were gone, Jesus struck up a conversation with a woman of questionable reputation. When the disciples came back, they found that He wasn't hungry. Why? Jesus explained: "I have meat to eat that you know not of. . . . My meat is to do the will of him that sent me, and to finish his work." (John 4:32,34) From the proper perspective, to witness to someone about the nature of God and find that many people in the community spontaneously turn to God as a result is more important than lunch. This is one meaning of fasting.

Jesus also addressed the issue of reputation with respect to surface religion. Early in the sermon He talked about superficial piety. The giving of "alms" for show received the reward of being noticed. It proved to be only an empty exercise. Also, prayers performed on public street corners were motivated by show. These prayers proved to be nothing but words chanted by men. Fasting, followed by intoned testimony about your professed action, may win you approbation from the shallow thinkers, but the real spiritual exercise of fasting is motivated by true desire to seek and do God's will. Hypocrites seek admiration for their superficial piety. "Verily, they have their reward." (Matthew 6)

One thing that bothers most of us is facing up to our eventual death. "Which of you by taking thought can add one cubit unto his stature?" (Matthew 6:27) Although there is controversy among the commentators about the meaning of this verse, many of them relate it to an Old Testament expression where length of life is measured in linear measure. (Psalm 39:5) Under these circumstances, Jesus is talking about adding to your span of life. Paraphrasing: "Who can add a moment to his life by worrying?" Most of my worries about tomorrow would lose much of their sting if I could solve the problem of the length of my life.

Back to the present momentarily: The fast pace of life in the USA creates many pressures. Since the recent death of my wife, Hattie, more people have been sharing their troubles with me. There are families in my community with severe economic pressures. There are homes that are plagued with alcohol and drug problems. There are homes where love seems dead. There are homes that are troubled by serious illness. Loneliness looms large in the lives of many of my friends. When someone close to me died, life took on new meaning. Food and drink as a way of life lost their appeal. Even much that previously passed for entertainment became hollow. Clothing lost its top billing and although I wanted to look neat, being the best-dressed man on the block was no longer meaningful. Visual righteousness for show became repulsive. Reasons for pious exercises became internalized. I feel impelled to make the most of every moment. When Hattie died, my physical mortality slapped me in the face.

Resuming my adventure: As I carefully read the sermon, Jesus told me not to worry about tomorrow. How can I implement His command? In the sermon, Jesus implied that I can minimize worrying by ordering my priorities. "Seek you first the kingdom of God . . ." (Matthew 6:33).

The first step in ordering my life was to determine the kingdom of God for me. It would be nice if I could have said that the kingdom of God was the church I was pastoring. However, Jesus rebuked the Pharisees for such an attitude. "The kingdom of God comes not with observation: Neither shall they say, Lo here! or lo there! for, behold the kingdom of God is within you." (Luke 17:20,21) I learned that the church as an organization was important in nurturing the kingdom of God, but was not to become a substitute for it. In order to determine the kingdom of God for me, I had to first surrender any right to my life. That was tough. I had to acknowledge that God had made me and also that He provided an escape from the tangle of my sins after I had taken control of my life and made a mess of it. When I admitted my need for Him to take control, I moved into a position to begin to see the kingdom of God within me.

I, like everyone else, am a unique individual. God has spent centuries developing only one of me. The same could be said of you. Therefore, He has a plan that will most effectively use my talents or your talents. When I had concurred with Him by telling Him that I was surrendering my control to Him, He began to help me develop along lines that continue to bring the most satisfaction to me and glory to Him. He did not revealed the full plan to me from the beginning. "We walk by faith not by sight." (2 Corinthians 5:7) Sometimes I have not been able to discern His working in events that involve me. But I have found that when I remain steady, proceeding under the last directions that I have received, I can go in confidence. Then, many times, in retrospect I can see that He really was directing my life even through the dark places.

My faith is still growing on the foundation of past experience. Seeing a pattern in the things from my own past helps me build confidence for the future. The more I live by faith, the more "real," things of spiritual value become to me. It was by this process that I began to lay up treasures for myself in heaven where moth and rust cannot destroy and thieves can't break in and steal. (Matthew 6:20). As my attention shifted to love, patience, gentleness, kindness, self-control, and similar attributes, I worried less about material things. I had become aware that I was steward of all that I seem to possess.

There were times when I was misunderstood as I follow God's call for my life. Many of my acquaintances talked about me when I left the pastoral ministry to teach in a secular university. I believe that God led me in the switch and, to the best of my ability, I am still pursuing the kingdom of God for my life.

Once I had ordered my priorities, I tried to let God develop me naturally. Jesus said: "Consider the lilies of the field, how they grow; they toil not, neither do they spin: And yet I say unto you, That even Solomon in all his glory was not arrayed like one of these." (Matthew 6:28,29). I am not a botanist but the developing of flowers seems to be very natural for a dandelion. I am quite sure that the yellow marvels that dot our lawns in the spring do so without any conscious effort.

Suppose I worry about something I have planted. I might do what one of my children did after he planted a bean one day. The next morning, he dug it up to see if it had sprouted. Since it hadn't, he replanted it. This process was repeated until finally he impatiently threw the bean into the garbage. So when I am worried about my spiritual growth, I tend to destroy the "mustard seed" of faith that was given to me when I surrendered to God. Under those circumstances, I am in danger of throwing away my confidence. (Hebrews 10:35)

Consider the amazing growth and development of a child. If the child eats nutritious foods, gets the needed rest, exercises in play and work, he or she has no need to worry about his or her physical development. Similarly, when I have fed my mind with thoughts of things that are honest, just, pure, of good report, I have sometimes found it possible to relax in the spirit. When I commune with God through prayer and praise, I have no need to worry about my spiritual development.

This does not mean that I will be immune to stresses. The circumstances of life often seem "unfriendly" and threaten my destruction. Consider the grass. It was used as fuel for the ovens. (Matt. 6:30) Its existence was transient but God developed it until it was ready to be used for man's benefit. All of us are also physical transients. God will help us to survive the storms of life until we can better serve His purpose on the other side."

Obviously, I survived my first pastorate. Here's how. We spent our first night in the lovely home of one of our church members. The next day, someone brought bedroom furniture out of their attic and barn for us to use. Another friend of the church loaned us their wicker porch furniture for our "living room." My mother had a table, a piano, and a buffet that we could use. A friend of the church hauled these pieces of furniture and helped us get them into the parsonage. A neighbor gave us an icebox, but we couldn't afford the ice so it didn't help much. The church bought a gas range for five dollars and we asked them to install it in the kitchen. We scrubbed the food off the ceiling where a pressure cooker explosion had deposited it. We washed the woodwork. The church bought paint and we painted the kitchen cabinets. Then the people of the church had a spaghetti supper at the parsonage and for entertainment, they papered the kitchen ceiling and walls down to the wainscot. We shut off the two bedrooms in need of repair. I built bookcases and was given a library table. I set up my study in one corner of the living room. We entertained the college quartet by seating them on table leaves supported by packing boxes.

The executive secretary of the National Holiness Association hired Hattie to work a couple hours a day as he needed help. With the added income we were eventually able to purchase a refrigerator for sixty dollars on the installment plan. My father-in-law called the district superintendent and told him about our car. He put us in touch with a loan company that refinanced our car. When we ran out of potatoes, a church member gave us a bag of graham flour and we could afford lard, so we ate biscuits for a while.

Hattie became sick with her pregnancy and had to stay in bed for a time. Our neighbors, all members of other denominations, were terrific. They brought in food. They helped with house cleaning and washing the dishes. We scraped enough money together to buy a ton of coal for the furnace. When the man delivered it and saw our plight, he brought us another load free of charge. We were invited to spend Christmas with some of our new friends who attended our church. Best of all, there was food. Hattie was ashamed of the amount of food that I ate.

A church of our denomination in another city brought us a "pounding." Then another church began to send us a small check each week. The pastor in the neighboring town was in difficult financial straits also, but he and his family gave us considerable spiritual support.

I tried to find work but was frustrated at every turn of the way. I tried to raise a garden. The potatoes were ruined by scab, the tomatoes died of blight, the carrots were riddled by nematodes, and nothing produced except the rhubarb which I hadn't planted and we couldn't eat because we couldn't afford the sugar. We did have some apples and pears from trees in the yard. I worked at trying to increase the size of the congregation. I established excellent community relations. I was elected president of the Ministerial Association. The weekly paper and the daily paper competed for "news" of my activities. The weekly paper printed everything I sent them, even the thank you notes. We had many friends, but it seemed that each had his own church.

When Hattie went to the hospital, the doctor charged a small fee and the hospital bill did not overwhelm us. It turned out that the baby had been destroyed by an abnormal growth of the placenta and although saddened by the events, we were aware that we did not have the means for child care at that time.

After two years, it seemed to us as though God had exhausted His source of surprises. We were still under financial pressure. My health was being threatened by malnutrition. One day I received a letter from my college roommate. He asked how things were going and wondered if I would be interested in moving to another pastorate. I found the money for postage and answered in the affirmative. After a "trial sermon," we were given the call and moved to a charge that really paid fifty dollars a week!

After seven years in this difficult situation, Sarah moved with her husband and son to a new community. This community was not so backward and the church was larger. The parsonage had electricity and central heat. The town had several stores along with a post office, high school and funeral home. It even had public transportation to the larger neighboring community. In a word, God moved them into a much better physical environment.

We hope that this excursion into our past to a time when God delivered Hattie and me and Sarah and her family from very difficult situations has encouraged you as much as it has us. Maybe this will stimulate your faith, as it has ours, to believe that God loves us and will provide a way for us to cope. Hattie and I still had the stars of idealism in our eyes but learned to live one real day at a time. Sarah learned that obedience to God does not promise an easy time but He has promised to be with us. Our priorities are ordered, to the best of our knowledge, according to the Scriptures. We are trying to maintain our confidence. God moves us when our mission is accomplished.

God loves us. May He deliver us from the severe trials of life and until He does, may He give us grace to live victoriously.

CHAPTER 13

PEACE IN TURMOIL

Summary: The peace of Christ is internal, faith-inspired, and heaven-sent. It is based on His teachings which are made credible by the fulfillment of His predictions. Jesus' disciples had peace that was a result of a new perspective, and a sense of adequacy. Their peace was maintained by the support of one another.

It looks like there is a cliff straight ahead (actually the next chapter) and I think I could use a little rest before we tackle it. Why don't we sit on this rock and think about peace? In a previous chapter, the one about worry, we talked about the "peace of God." While we are "resting," let's think about peace as Jesus perceived it.

Do you remember that the Messiah was called the "Prince of Peace"? (Isaiah 9:7). Well, when Jesus was born, His birth was announced to the shepherds with a message of "peace on earth. . ." (Luke 2:14). Much later when His death was imminent Jesus said to his disciples: "Peace I leave with you, my peace I give unto you: not as the world gives, give I unto you. Let not your heart be troubled neither let it be afraid." (John 14:27).

What do you suppose that He meant by "My peace?" For a long time, I thought of peace as a picture of a pleasant environment with all my physical wants satisfied, having no pain, having every-thing determined by my dictates, and having nothing to worry about. But Jesus concept was obviously different. He explained to His disciples: "These things I have spoken unto you, that in me you might have peace In the world, you will have tribulation but be of good cheer, I have overcome the world." (John 16:33). What are some of the things that He had been talking about?

First, He told them that they would be misunderstood by the religious community. (John 16:2) It was to be violent. The disci-ples would be excommunicated from the synagogues. The situa-tion would worsen until some who would try to kill Christ's followers would think that they were doing God a favor.

Christ was leaving them. (John 16:20). The manner in which Christ would take His departure was to be extremely difficult for them. The disciples would lament, feel defeated and confused. Their enemies would be delighted, feel triumphant and vindi-cated. The world would believe that Christ's departure was proof that they were right and Christ was an impostor. (That would be hard for me to take!) There would be some surprises. The disci-ples would have their sorrow replaced by joy. They might not understand all the implications of these events immediately, but their joy would be more permanent than transient.

A new manifestation of God would be in the form of the Holy Spirit. (John 16:7). This would usher in a new era. God's revela-tion would not be limited to a select few but would be available to all who would meet the conditions for receiving the Holy Spirit. The bodily presence of Christ would be removed so that the special presence of God would be delocalized.

Because of this they would have peace? Obviously, the peace He had in mind was not the cessation of all hostilities. As a matter of fact, He promised explicitly that they would experience tribula-tion. Tribulation may be due to physical circumstances, social isolation, or psychological stress or all of the above. The peace of Christ is internal, faith-inspired and heaven-sent and therefore does not depend upon the state of your health or your environment.

Jesus indicated that they would have peace because His teachings would be made credible by the fulfillment of his predictions. This entire discourse had to do with a new relationship with God. There would be less support for their faith from things that are tangible and visible. There would be a greater necessity to rely on the words of Jesus and appropriate the truth by faith. They would need considerable evidence that Jesus was the Christ as He claimed before they could accept this new aspect of the divine revelation. Jesus succinctly expressed His theology: "I came forth from the Father, (His divine origin), and am come into the world, (His incarnation), again, I leave the world, (His death), and go to the Father, (His resurrection and ascension)." (John 16:28). It was important that His disciples believed this if they were to face tribulation without the support of the physical presence of Jesus.

Since Jesus had told them what to expect, they would have peace because they could be confident that God is not taken by surprise. I remember an occasion that my two-year-old son needed a shot. Hattie took him to the doctor's office. On the way she told him that the doctor would pinch his arm a little and he would feel a little pin prick. When it was his turn for the shot, he flinched but didn't cry because he knew what to expect. Since his mother had told him in advance what to expect, he felt confident that she was in control of the situation. It hurt some, but his mother had permitted it and so it must be all right. I need to know that God was not taken by surprise by Hattie's cancer and death. What about your problems? Sarah mumbled, "I sure hope God was not taken by surprise by my losing my job."

The disciples did not always properly interpret the events as they occurred. Jesus predicted that each of them would forsake Him as the events progressed. (John 16:32). They did. When Jesus was arrested in the garden, the disciples abandoned Him. Later Peter and John entered the court to see what was going on. When each of the apostles realized what he had done, he remembered the prediction of Jesus. Each of them, except Judas, repented and was restored. Judas, who was absent during this discourse, later gave up in despair and committed suicide. Each one believed in Jesus' love because He had warned them in advance.

When Jesus was crucified, his disciples failed to grasp the significance of it. Later they would remember that Jesus had said repeatedly that He was leaving. They thought that they had understood what He meant. Perhaps they thought that Jesus would leave this world like Elijah did. When He died, they were confused. Many of their enemies were happy. These enemies, convinced that they were right, challenged Jesus to prove them wrong by coming down from the cross.

His resurrection also took everyone by surprise. When the women reported that they had seen angels who told them about the resurrection of Jesus, it seemed as though they were making up stories. (Luke 24:11). Peter and John went to the garden and found the tomb empty but were puzzled by it. John almost grasped the significance of it when he noticed the way the shroud was lying. Even when they saw Him, they were frightened because there was something different about Him. He entered the locked room without opening the door. To prove to the apostles that He was not an apparition, He ate some food while they watched.

Following Jesus' instructions, the disciples waited in Jerusalem. After a business meeting in which they elected someone to take Judas' place, they waited and prayed for the "promise of the Father". (Acts 1:4). Just as Jesus had promised, the Holy Spirit was given to all who were in the group. They were excited about this. It seems that they were beginning to catch on to what Jesus meant in some of His predictions. This was the "Spirit of truth; whom the world cannot receive, because it sees him not, neither knows him: but you know him; for he dwells with you, and shall be in you." (John 14:17).

It wasn't long until the beatings came. After the advent of the giving of the Holy Spirit, called the *Paraclete*, the apostles had a new boldness. Their straightforward preaching caused them to clash with the temple authorities. At first, Peter and John were imprisoned overnight. They were then threatened and released.

Later they were taken into custody again. This time they were beaten before they were released. Evidently they were prepared for this because they rejoiced that they were counted worthy to suffer for the sake of their faith in Jesus. (Acts 5:41).

Martyrdom soon followed as predicted. James, John's brother, was the first of the apostles to be killed for his faith. (Acts 12:2). Earlier, a disciple named Stephen had been stoned to death by a group of religious people. (Acts 7:54-60).

In many of the cases mentioned above, the apostles were taken by surprise. Jesus had tried to prepare them, but they didn't understand until after the fact. Then they could look back and be assured that God had not been taken by surprise, but was in control, allowing only that which could be transformed into good for His servants.

It appears that their peace was a result of a new perspective. The apostles were ordinary men. They had lived in this world and seemed to have given no consideration to the fact that there might be another. Being successful in business was what really mattered. When they followed Jesus, most of them seemed to think that they were in on the ground floor of a political revolution that would topple the Roman government or at least win freedom from that government for the Jews. It was especially important to impress Jesus. They argued over who was the greatest, who had the most ability to govern, who would have the most power when Jesus took over. Each one wanted to be the greatest in the new regime.

Later, new attitudes are evident from Peter's letter. Here are some excerpts from his letter. "Blessed be the God and Father of our Lord Jesus Christ, which according to his abundant mercy has begotten us again unto a lively hope by the resurrection of Jesus Christ from the dead, to an inheritance incorruptible . . . reserved in heaven for you who are kept by the power of God through faith unto salvation ready to be revealed in the last time. . . . Seeing you have purified your souls in obeying the truth through the Spirit unto unfeigned love of the brethren, love one another with a pure heart fervently: being born again, not of corruptible seed, but of incorruptible, by the word of God, which lives and abides forever. For all flesh is as grass and all the glory of man as the flower of grass. The grass withers and the flower thereof falls away, but the word of the Lord endures forever." (1 Peter 1:3-5;22-25).

"The elders which are among you I exhort . . . feed the flock of God which is among you, taking oversight . . . not for filthy lucre, . . . neither being lords over God's heritage, but being examples to the flock." (1 Peter 5:1-3).

To me, these excerpts are "hard evidence" that Peter, as the spokesman for the apostles, developed a new outlook on life. The "real world" is the incorruptible one that is invisible at the present time. The physical is transient. The spiritual nature of love out of a pure heart is eternal. Striving for glory among men is vain because it is perishable, like a withering bouquet. Even in the exercise of legitimate authority, one is to lead by example in humility.

Their peace was a result of a sense of adequacy. Jesus had said, "Be of good cheer; I have overcome the world." The apostles had observed Jesus' life for about three years. As Jesus had faced the waves on the Sea of Galilee, He had proven to be master of the winds and sea. As he faced a demented man, He had proven to be master of human personality gone awry. As He faced the crowds, He had proven to be master of presenting the truth. Even when a little girl had died, He had proven to be master of the situation and brought her back to life.(Luke 8). Then He died! He was tried in a Roman court and found "Not guilty!" Even so, He was killed as a common criminal. Most of His apostles had forsaken Him by this time. John initially left Him in the garden, but came back to observe. John saw Jesus die on the cross. Jesus had indeed overcome the world in the case of natural phenomena, psychological problems, and communication. But now?

Perhaps doubts ran through John's mind as he saw Jesus dying on the cross. The words kept running around in John's head, "These thing I have told you that you might have peace. . . .

I have overcome the world." Is this all part of a larger scene? Could Jesus' vision have included this? "I came into this world from the Father and now I am going to return to the Father." Was this included in the deeper meaning? "I will not leave you without help. I will come to you." "John, take care of my mother." How could all this fit into a pattern? To one of the criminals that was crucified at the same time He said: "Today you will be with me in paradise." Jesus seemed to be in charge until His agonizing cry: "My God, My God, Why have you forsaken me?" Were we all mistaken? A final expression seemed to ameliorate the cry of agony. "Father, into your hands I commit my spirit." "My peace I give to you!" — Hmm — With the passing of time, perhaps he will understand the significance of these statements and events.

Fear settled down on the little group of apostles. They huddled together with a few friends in a room with the door barred. (John 20:19). The peace of God seemed to allude them. They were startled by the appearance of the risen Christ. Even this did not bring the promised peace. Their emotions, like their minds, were confused. Gradually the things that "He had spoken unto them" began to take on deeper meaning. What He had said about their lament turning into joy was being accomplished in their experience.

What is the most frightening and powerful thing in the world? Death is inevitable, coming to every person and thus is powerful. Death presents us with an element of the unknown and thus is frightening. Jesus had experienced death as a condemned man even though He was found innocent by the Roman court. He was young and that made His death seem more tragic. But death could not defeat Him. He conquered death by His resurrection. He had indeed overcome the world. Now He holds the keys of death and hell. (Revelation 1:18). The sting of death is sin. (I Corinthians 15:56). Because He has conquered death, Jesus now has the power and authority to deal with the sin problem in the life of anyone who will allow Him to take control of his life. This brings peace. "Therefore, being justified by faith, we have peace with

God through our Lord Jesus Christ." (Romans 5:1). This is the essence of the peace that Jesus gives.

The Holy Spirit was revealed in a special sense on the Day of Pentecost. He came as the Helper that Jesus had promised. His coming helped the apostles by bringing all things to their remembrance that Jesus had said to them. (John 14:26). With this came a new sense of being able to successfully handle any circumstance. Nothing could defeat them. Jesus had overcome the world and now He was able to help them and strengthen them through the presence of the Holy Spirit. Even death was no longer considered defeat. They remembered that Jesus had said, "Because I live, you shall live also." (John 14:19). His resurrection had guaranteed their immortality. They could not be defeated. They were indestructible.

When the disciples met with difficult circumstances or tribulations, they trusted the promise of Jesus that prayer made grace available. Fellowship with God took on a new meaning. "If you ask anything in My name, I will do it." (John 14:14). Talking with God was no longer an empty formality but a vital reality. When they needed help in some situation, they asked for it. Since they had a new sense of fellowship with God, He didn't seem so remote.

The peace that Jesus gave them was reinforced by the support of one another. Jesus had told them not to be surprised if the world hated them because it hated Him and His Father. In the midst of these trying circumstances, they were commanded to love one another. (John 15:17). This group support would give them the strength they needed to present a united front to the world and pursue their goals with peace of soul.

Jesus had used the illustration of a vine to describe the new relationship that He and his disciples would have. "I am the vine, you are the branches." (John 15:5). They were to be productive because of the support they would get from the knowledge of His love for them and their love for one another.

Peter and John were very different personalities. Peter was impetuous. John was pensive. Early accounts indicate that they were companions in the ministry for some time and supported each other with their strengths. Peter did the talking. John did the thinking. Neither seemed worried about who would get the most credit. When Peter and John were released from prison they returned to the group of disciples. After they reported what had happened to them, the group "lifted up their voices to God with one accord." (Acts 4:24). Love was working to build a cooperative group, presenting a united front against the world without divisive competition within the group.

The peace that Jesus promised and the disciples received was not an ephemeral emotion. It was not a fleeting sense of satisfaction. It was not based on external circumstances. It was not a result of each of them having his own way. Instead it was a steady confidence that nothing would be able to ultimately frustrate their purpose. They were totally committed to God and His plan. They had confessed their sins and found forgiveness with God. God's Spirit was in control at the center of their lives. In happy circumstances or in tribulation, in life or in death, they would glorify God. If we can appropriate this peace it should help us as we face the cliff of "natural questions" immediately ahead of us.

All this may seem remote and foreign to us. These men lived years before the rush of modern society. They did not know the stress of jet-lag and computer frustration. They did not need to cope with noisy radios nor persuasive TV ads. Abbreviated schedules did not worry them. So, is this peace available to us in this age? Can we find the strength we need to meet life's demands in this twenty-first century?

During this Bible Study, Jim and Susie have been increasingly animated. When I posed these questions they both started talking at once. "Yes it is and we can." Then Susie let Jim go first. Their excitement was that they had a good example of this peace in their son, Arthur. Jim began to relate what he and Susie had been thinking.

"Arthur is now fifteen and living on three years of borrowed time. (Remember the prognosis was at the outside limit Arthur would live to be twelve.) I believe that part of the reason he is still alive is his attitude and perspective on life. Instead of focusing on what he doesn't have, he constantly thinks about what he does have. For example, he loves sports. There is no way now that he can participate by joining the team. But during the fall football season, he will be at the stadium for every home game. On a rainy day when he wakes up on the morning, he will say to his mother, 'You're not going to make me go to school in this terrible weather, are you? I will get sick and die!' But she makes him go anyway unless he is actually physically sick. On Friday night, however, even if the weather has turned cold and it is raining. He is excited at the supper table.

'What's the excitement, Arthur?'

'This is Friday night and the Bruins are having a home game.'

'But look at the weather, the temperature is near freezing and it is raining.'

'I'm going to the game! You can bundle me up and I will stay warm.'

'Really, it would be wise for you to stay home.'

'I'm going to the game!' Arthur says with a sense of finality.

He can't participate on the field, but he is one of the most avid supporters of the team.

"On the state level he is just as loyal to the State University even though we are fans of the Aggie University. One time we wanted to take him to an Aggie game and he resisted with, 'But what if I died? Could God find me there?' His upbeat spirit is fed by a strong faith in God."

Susie picks up the story. "Then too, he has faced death. He has been aware of the doctor's prognosis for quite some time but was determined to outlive the prediction and he has. He even jokes about death. If we make him do something that he doesn't want to do, (like sending him to school in the rain) he jokingly says, 'This weather is going to make me sick. — or whatever we want him to do — You may as well call the funeral home.' One day a friend was joking with Arthur. He reacted by holding his breath. Then in a breathless voice says, 'Take me to the hospital, can't you see I'm dying?' He obviously has come to grips with his own mortality."

Jim tells of Arthur's sense of adequacy. "The Muscular Dystrophy Group provided a motorized wheelchair for Arthur to use. This has been a real boon for him. It gives him an independence that increases his sense of adequacy. The wheelchair has a safety belt but Arthur wouldn't use it. One day he was in the backyard and hit a small hole that made the chair lurch. He tumbled out onto the lawn. A neighbor saw the whole thing and came to his rescue. Reluctantly, since then, he fastens his safety belt. Interestingly though, he never mentioned the incident to us. The only way we found out about it was from the neighbor. He rides around the subdivision in his chair. There is a cemetery about two blocks from our house and he often goes there, apparently to think and to talk with God. He is at peace when he returns."

Sarah asks, "What about Ken?"

"What do you mean?"

"How does Ken interact with his brother?"

"Oh," Susie replies, "They act like brothers. Sometimes they fight, sometimes they play together and sometimes they work on their work together. It is a normal relationship — just like any good sibling relationship."

I observe. "Your family is to Arthur what the rest of the apostles were to John. You are in this together as family. Except where necessary, Arthur is not treated differently because of his disease. He is disciplined. He is loved. He has his chores. He is allowed to express his feelings and opinions. He is allowed to interact with the family just like Ken. With this group support, the rough things are bearable and the good times are enjoyable."

Isabelle, who has been listening closely, says softly, "Thanks. Your description of Arthur and his peace has helped me think about my life. I will pray for a new perspective and sense of adequacy. You have made me aware an aspect of my relationship with Christ that I have not taken advantage of — a prayer for peace."

Larry added, "Just like He promised, God has given me His Spirit when I humbled myself and ask Him. I committed my life to Him and asked Him to take full control. At that time, I experienced an incredible sense of peace. Then when Cynthia left, I felt empty again. Through this discussion, I have come to realize that peace is not a surface emotion, but a deep sense of the 'rightness' of things. I have a sense of adequacy now because I know that God is in control. He is not taken by surprise. Sharing in this group has helped me realize that I am not alone. I can go on now even though the climb may be steep."

Sarah thanked Jim and Susie for their comments. Her eyes are sparkling with a new confidence. "I believe that I will soon be finding a job. I believe that God, Who has furnished a place for me and Mike to stay, will furnish the means for me to pay my share. I have peace now in hope."

Come on, let's tackle the cliff!

CHAPTER 14

NATURAL QUESTIONS WAITING FOR SUPERNATURAL ANSWERS

Summary: How do we handle sickness, death, disaster, and grief? The prophet was told to wait for the answer and he waited expectantly. The answer that came was surprising — "the just shall live by his faith." This does not deny the existence of evil, but the "just" man pursues his life of right living in spite of evil circumstances. He can do this even in the face of physical death because his experiential knowledge of God assures him of immortality.

This cliff, the problem of evil, is a formidable barrier to health. If we don't have any help, we might not make it. However, even though we may not fully understand the answer to the "why" of life, I am confident that we will surmount this barrier and be on our way to mental health again.

Jim suggests that we examine the cliff first. The group responds immediately.

"Notice the natural disasters. There are earthquakes that often kill thousands of people. Sometimes the earthquake is on the ocean floor resulting in a disastrous tsunami. And what about hurricanes and tornadoes? Then there are recent news reports of active volcanoes in various parts of the globe which have caused much damage and death. In the past couple of years there have been floods covering large areas of different countries. We also think about the damaging mudslides. There are also wildfires that destroy much property and wildlife."

"Notice also the inhumane human activities. Totalitarian rulers imprison or murder their rivals. Often the group with the upper hand endeavors genocide under the politically correct 'ethnic cleansing' label. In either case there are mass murders with bulldozed common graves."

"Yes, and what about the terrorists? Remember Oklahoma City. The government handling of the Waco situation supposedly led to that. But then there was New York City twin towers of the World Trade Center and the Washington terrorist attack on the Pentagon. Who knows what prompted those attacks?"

"What about the schools? Students killing other students and teachers."

"Or young people wasting themselves on drugs."

Isabelle speaks up and says, "Let me get personal. Although I am a Christian and try to foster my relationship with God, this trip into the canyon (especially the deep pit of clinical depression) has brought me face to face with this problem. The cliff is very real to me. I thought that I could avoid it by ignoring it. I became suicidal. Maybe we can help each other as we try to make our way over this obstacle."

Michelle adds her problem. "Nearly every night I wonder if I did the right thing. I wanted to stay for my children's sake. Andy became so violent that I was afraid that he would carry out his threats. Maybe I should have let him beat me senseless or kill me. I am glad that I was not frightened out of my faith in Jesus. The problem of evil has a personal touch for me."

I will tell my story. One Wednesday night after class, I started to shake violently from chills. My temperature went to 102 plus and refused to come down below 101 in spite of all the medication that my doctor and I could imagine to use. Consequently my doctor checked me into the hospital on Saturday night. I spent a week there with antibiotics and other treatment. So, two and a half years after the death of my wife, I had time to think about the great questions that had been nagging me since that time. I believe that there is a vision for this present time.

I discovered the little book of Habakkuk, one of the Minor Prophets. He is helping me. He moaned: "O Lord, how long shall I cry, and You will not hear! even cry out unto You of violence, and You will not save! Why do You show me iniquity, and cause me to behold grievance? For spoiling and violence are before me: and there are those that raise up strife and contention. Therefore the law is slack and judgment never goes forth: for the wicked compass about the righteous; therefore wrong judgment proceeds." (Habakkuk 1:2-4).

To bring this into our context, let me paraphrased this wail thus: "O Lord, how long will our hearts bleed and our minds reel from the blows of sickness and death, from the life-shattering tragedies that have floored us? Not only did my wife die, but others have been cut down in their prime. The university student who was an active, Christian influence among her friends was killed by senseless cancer. Isabelle is devastated by clinical depression. Michelle plagued with guilt over her leaving her family even though she had no choice. Arthur, young and innocent, Jim and Susie's child, stricken with a debilitating illness and dying in front of his parents' eyes for about ten years now. Is there no meaning in life? Will disease and death reign forever?"

I spent six weeks this summer with some eminent biologists. Some of them thought that they had the answer. "We are creatures of mindless chance." It seemed strange to me that as a group we were trying to move away from the data plane of phenomena to constructs that would allow us to form a broad picture of order in the enormous mass of biological data that continues to grow. If we are simply the result of mindless chance, why look for evidence of order or intelligent design?

There is some evidence that the prophet Habakkuk became skeptical when many of the people in his native Judah were becoming openly wicked and violent. His fellow citizens had a long history of a covenantal relationship with God. They were thought of as "God's Chosen People." God is holy and therefore His people are to be holy. If so, why should the wicked prosper in his country? This problem had been addressed before. In many of his prayers the psalmist cried for deliverance from the snares of the wicked. In one psalm we are urged to "Fret not yourself because of evil doers, neither be envious against the workers of iniquity. . . . I have seen the wicked in great power, and spreading himself like a green bay tree. Yet he passed away, and, lo, he was not: yea, I sought him, but he could not be found." (Psalm 37:1,35,36).

Then Habakkuk learned that the Lord was going to punish the wrong doers by allowing the country to be captured by a foreign nation. . "For, lo, I raise up the Chaldeans, that bitter and hasty nation, which shall march through the breadth of the land, to possess the dwelling places that are not theirs." (Habakkuk 1:6). This was not an acceptable solution as far as the prophet could see. It only compounded the question. The Chaldeans were ruthless, arrogant, idolatrous, and heathen. God was "of purer eyes than to behold evil, and cannot look on iniquity: wherefore do You look upon them that deal treacherously, and hold Your tongue when the wicked devour the man that is more righteous than he?" (Habakkuk 1:13). Surely the worse man in Judah was better then any of these heathen in this swift and terrible army.

Habakkuk decided that the only way to get an answer was to persist in prayer. The questions raised were too important to ignore. There was no way to find help from his contemporaries. He was not willing to pose these questions even to the nationally known prophet Jeremiah. He decided to go straight to God. This was a bold and dangerous move, but God honored his honesty. The prophet had faith that God was interested in helping him solve the problem.

When the Lord spoke to the prophet, He indicated that there was indeed a vision that would help him to see more clearly the working of the Lord. The promised vision could be simply put and quickly grasp. The prophet was to be prepared to share it with others. He was told to "Write the vision, and make it plain upon the tablets." (Habakkuk 2:2). There is indeed a vision for those troubled times but the vision might not come as soon as expected. God said "Wait for it!" (Habakkuk 2:3).

Wait? Hanging suspended in space part-way up the cliff? How contrary to our way of life! We are conditioned to expect everything given to us with little effort on our part. We are further conditioned to expect things instantly. Even some of our schools teach immediate gratification by example. I am frustrated sometimes by the people who can't read the sign on the moving walkways in some airports. It clearly says: "Walk left, stand right." Sometimes people block the whole walk-way so that I can't walk. Often when I get to the gate, I must wait until they start boarding my plane. Our fast-paced lives continue to accelerate. Perhaps we not only need to wait, but learn how to wait.

There are many ways to wait. You have no doubt seen someone wait impatiently. The announcement comes over the PA, "Flight 766 is delayed because of mechanical difficulties." As minutes stretch into hours, some people pace the floor, look at their watches every 30 seconds and hound the agent frequently for the latest word. Frustration grows until they are rude to nearly everyone around them. Have you ever been frustrated in waiting for God? You believe His promise that the vision will come, but wonder why the delay. I have a tendency to want to know, to ask questions and seek answers. I have been guilty of asking why something that I have prayed earnestly for does not occur according to my timetable.

Closely related to the impatient waiter, is the resentful one. This person was raised permissively. Tantrums have been rewarded by desired action. Now that he is an adult, the behavior pattern is only slightly modified. When it comes to religion, he demands things from God and dictates the timetable. When God is God and does not pamper his whim, he turns from God and resentfully remarks: "I never did think there was anything to this religion stuff anyway!"

In contrast to those mentioned above is the person who waits resignedly. The attitude conveyed by this person seems to be that of indifference. When he is told that he must wait, he reads a book, goes to sleep, or plays video games. He doesn't seem to care whether what he must wait for comes or not. God says "Wait for a vision," and so the resigned waiter turns his attention to other interests and seems to forget the questions that prompted him to approach God in the first place.

Habakkuk was not one to turn his interest elsewhere. He declared, "I will stand upon my watch, and set me upon the tower, and will watch to see what he will say unto me." (Habakkuk 2:1) This is the attitude of expectant waiting. The questions in the prophet's mind were too urgent to casually wait, turning his attention to something else in the meantime. It reminds me of Christmas. We have a rule in our house that everyone must have showered and dressed before anyone can open any presents. As the daddy of the clan, I am usually the last one ready. As the children, although they are now adults, are waiting there is an excitement in the air. Something wonderful is about to happen.

The excitement mounts as Habakkuk climbs onto his prayer tower. He is about to hear from God! God honors his faith and gives him an answer. The first part of the message is a bit garbled in the transmission, but seems to mean that the proud, self-reliant person will not be able to stand in the coming storm. However, the last part of the message comes through loud and clear. "THE JUST SHALL LIVE BY HIS FAITH." (Habakkuk 2:4). In a time when religion was a matter of a nation's relation with its God, this message was novel. It indicated that the individual was responsible for his own actions. A vital message for today when the tendency is to try to blame circumstances or social conditions for our behavior.

This message differentiates between the just and the unjust. This implies some standard of right and wrong. It strikes a blow at relativism. The illusion of relativism is not new. In the days of the Judges of Israel, it is recorded that "every man did that which was right in his own eyes." (Judges 21:25). That attitude toward right and wrong continues to appear even in our day. For example, it is not uncommon to hear someone say, "If it feels good, do it." Also, some people will perform acts of vandalism in the name of "right."

Evil is real. Evil has invaded our world. The righteous suffer. God suffers! Even though He is infinite and omnipotent, He has chosen to accept limits. Deliberately, He created man, giving him the capacity to love and the ability to choose the object of his love. Since man chose to disobey God in the Garden of Eden, proneness to evil has become part of our inheritance.

God is infinite in all aspects of His character and nature. As a result, He can have knowledge of something without experiencing it. Man, by contrast, is finite and can know something only by experience. Man analyses, synthesizes, organizes, and interprets his experience. By use of his imagination, a person can combine certain elements of his experience in various ways to attain "new knowledge" but this is still limited by experience. When I read a book, I interpret it against the background of my experience. Suppose I had never seen frozen water. I have experienced sensations of "coldness," "solidity," "transparency," and other related abstractions from phenomena and therefore would be able to imagine what ice is like.

When the "serpent" suggested that eating the forbidden fruit would make them as the gods "knowing good and evil," (Genesis 3:5), he falsely suggested that man could expand his realm of knowledge to infinity. He also suggested that man had the right to define what is good and what is evil for him. Man should take control of his own destiny. He should be his own sovereign. A more subtle implication is that God did not want what is best for mankind. Accordingly, man knows better than God what is good for him. God is not to be trusted in areas concerned with the ideal human situation. He is only worried about maintaining His authority and preserving His image. However, the result of accepting the "serpent's" suggestion was an experience that was degenerating in that it was contrary to the true nature of man. As a result of this degeneration, man has become limited in his ability to discern good from evil, an effect opposite from the one that he sought.

This limited ability to judge what is good for us, sometimes even in the most trivial of cases, coupled with our free choice allows us to make mistakes and suffer the consequences even though we are totally committed to doing God's will. The negative consequences that sometimes follow cause us to grapple with the question "Why do I, though totally committed to doing God's will, suffer?"

Some things that are evil by nearly any standard can sometimes issue in some common good. For example, King David's affair with Bathsheba would be condemned in nearly any society. One of the children born to that union was Solomon, the wise man who became king of Israel upon the death of his father. (2 Samuel 11,12; 1 Kings 1,3).

To accommodate these phenomena, man has invented the organizing principle of relativism. The fundamental idea in this philosophy is that there are no absolutes. Each individual is motivated by the idea that he or she is the one who decides what is good or evil for him or her. Every event and response is judged in its context according to that individual's "standard." For example, some people argue that taking a piece of property that rightfully belongs to someone else is justified if the owner is a corporation.

Another aspect of the problem of evil is related to the fact that each of us is a part of the human society. "No man is an island." As such, we experience the good and the bad that are common to our involvement in humanity. For example, I may get lung cancer as a result of inhaling cigarette smoke even though I have never personally smoked a cigarette. On the other hand, I can help my body to overcome prostatitis by the use of an antibiotic that I did not formulate.

The personification of evil, for example, as "the serpent," "Satan," "the devil," has broader implications than simply human choice. Man chose to disobey God by declaring himself sovereign and deciding what was good and evil. This choice also influenced nature in general. God said, ". . . cursed is the ground for your sake" (Genesis 3:17). This might explain why evolution seems to be a random walk instead of proceeding according to design. This also helps us to understand the apparent aberrations that challenge the concept of harmony in nature.

The "just" or "righteous one" appears to refer to that person who attempts to discern the right and pursue a course of action dictated by that understanding. Such a person shall live. In desperate times, it seems that many such persons are killed along with the unrighteous. Evidently there is some deeper meaning to the word "live." The prophet seemed to glimpse the immortality of the soul. There is another realm where the just will live in the presence of a righteous God.

There is another sense in which the "just shall live by his faithfulness." When times are turbulent, those who look to the material world for stability are afraid. Their world is apparently fragile in the face of the "invading hordes." The ill-gotten wealth which has given meaning to their life is about to be taken away. The "just" person, by contrast, derives meaning for his life from the principles of right living. By continuing faithfully to follow these principles, "living by faith," that person will be able to experience stability in an environment of turmoil.

As I lay in that hospital bed, I began to realize that the meaning in my life was not dependent upon the hectic pace of my active life. Perhaps the amount of action that I was crowding into my life was an attempt to forget. Maybe I was trying to deny the existence of the problems for which I had no solutions. I decided that true meaning in my life is to be found in my relationship with God. If I continue to pursue the development of this aspect of my life, I will find stability in spite of the frustration caused by the difficulty of the questions with which I struggle. This neither denies the reality of the problems nor the severity of my struggle to solve the problems.

Isabelle has become pensive. "It has helped me to see my problem in a different light. I am glad that I was able to admit that I had a problem and seek medical help. Also my counselor helped me to sort things out some. This trip is helping me to see that my trusting people was not wrong. Also, the way they deceived me was beyond my control. My problem was that I took the whole situation personally. I now have a new perspective in which the evil of others will affect me but I am protected in my inner core by my faith in and relationship with God. To surmount this cliff I don't need to know the solution to the "problem of evil" but to look to God Who is in control. By this faith, I shall live."

Michelle speaks up. "My feeling of guilt over whether I made the right choice or not is in the past. I can't change it now. There is no return. If the choice was correct, I must accept the consequences. If it was the wrong choice, I must leave it in the hands of a loving heavenly Father. With this newfound insight, I can now move on with my life and deal with the problems that lie ahead. As the Psalmist said, 'I will trust and not be afraid.' (Psalm 56:11)."

A principle of biblical interpretation seems to be that of evolving meaning. This is illustrated by the message that Habakkuk received. The immediate connotation was that the just would continue to pursue his life by being faithful to the religious principles that had ordered his life until this time. Regardless of the environmental circumstances, the righteous person would continue to do right as he understood it and allow God to control the consequences. The writer of the Hebrews picks up on this theme and pursues it. (Hebrews 10:38). He encourages his readers to remain faithful in the face of persecution and not to throw away their confidence. He adds a warning for those who "shrink back."

This was given a different connotation by the apostle Paul. (See Romans 1:17 and Galatians 3:11). Paul in his Roman letter extends the meaning to include life directed by belief in the righteousness of God. To the Galatians, he emphasizes the need of living by faith in contrast to attempting to obtain righteousness by keeping the law completely. This use of the word "faith" seems to imply an experiential knowledge of God and an identification with Christ and He with us. When we live by this kind of faith in Christ, we are "children of God." (Galatians 3:26). This has been historically interpreted as the answer to the problem of sin. Martin Luther and John Wesley had similar leaps of insight in interpreting this Scripture.

This brings me to a disturbing thought: Am I recommitting the original sin? Adam and Eve sought knowledge of good and evil from a source that God had expressly forbidden. They did not trust God. I am seeking knowledge so that I can explain the mysteries of good and evil in the world. Based on this knowledge, I can judge individual incidents with respect to whether they are good or bad. There seems to be a frightening parallel here. What am I to do? Remain ignorant, quit thinking, cop out? If so, why did God give me a mind and the drive to know? I believe that I am supposed to go as far as I can by my reason. I am to read, contemplate, search diligently for answers to tough questions just as Habakkuk did. Through it all, however, I must learn to trust the wisdom and goodness of God.

After Habakkuk received this message, he became confident that God would ultimately deliver His people. There would no doubt be tough times ahead. Because of the captivity there would be extreme hardship. He visualized pain, suffering, hunger and poverty. The prospects make him tremble. But, because of the message, he concludes his book with the statement that he will "rejoice in the God of his salvation." He acknowledges God as the source of his strength. (Habakkuk 3:18f).

Look, we have made it to the top of the cliff. All of our questions are not answered, but God has helped us to surmount the problem in our personal lives. It appears to be a gentle slope to the mesa of mental health, but there is a monster in our way. It appears that we must deal with anger before we are well.

CHAPTER 15

ANGER AND FORGIVENESS

Summary: *Anger is a common experience that is dangerous to ignore. It occurs when we are denied something that we feel that we are entitled to. It also may occur when we feel like we are losing control. If someone we love is hurt, we become angry. The resolution of anger is forgiveness. Forgiveness works for resolving some "hurt" that we have experienced. Forgiveness is an act of will. To be forgiven, we must be forgiving.*

You are right. We will need to overcome the monster before we can get back up on the mesa. The monster, anger, appears in a variety of emotional forms that are related. It covers the relatively tame emotion that is a ripple of irritation due to some unexpected difficulty. At the other extreme there is the life-threatening, uncontrollable emotional beast known as rage due to some threatening affront. Anger attacks a person's emotions much as a virus infects a person's physical body. It is usually accompanied by jealousy, frustration, fear, disappointment, depression, hatred and self-pity.

Most of us feel that we are entitled to certain things. When we are denied those things, often we respond in anger. For example, Cain was "wroth," (being interpreted as very angry) with his brother Abel because Abel's sacrifice was accepted and Cain's was not. Apparently, Cain felt that he was entitled to God's favor as much as Abel was. (Genesis 4:3 - 8).

When my late wife, Hattie, first was diagnosed as having cancer, I was allowed to see the x-ray. Later when tests were run, I was allowed to see some of the pathological reports if I asked. When her second bout with cancer occurred, I was informed about the exploratory surgery. The highly skilled surgeon had just completed operating on my wife. Being a man of compassion, he came to the waiting room and called me out so that we could talk in private. "The offending shadow on the chest x-ray came from a malignant tumor. I believe that I removed it all, but in so doing I had to sacrifice the nerve that controls a region of the left diaphragm." But, when the final bout with cancer began, the doctors ran another battery of tests. The doctor that was in charge of the case seemed to be secretive. I asked to see the pathological report and his temper flared. "Why do you want to see the report?" "It is my wife and I am intelligent enough to understand large portions of the report." I was angry. I felt that I was entitled to the information that Dr. Krim (not his real name) was with-holding. It made me suspicious that he was hiding something that I should know. When we returned for an appointment the next week, he asked meekly, "Do you want to see the pathological report now?" I answered, "No." I couldn't help but wonder what he had done to "clean up" the report.

Isabelle now has her Ph.D. in psychology and is a profes-sional psychologist. She is working for the state and thus must interact with many who do not have her skills or training. When she uses a battery of tests to assess an individual's potential or diagnose a problem, she expects the results to be considered in the treatment of the individual. Also, because of her training, she expects to consulted in planning the therapy or to devise a plan for the individual to become a productive citizen. There have been times when the political maneuvering is frustrating. Sometimes her supervisor asks that she "manipulate" some of the test results because it would mean more government money for the program. Isabelle is understandably angry. She believes that because of her training and experience that she is entitled to a certain amount of respect. Also, she is angry because they have essentially insulted her sense of values. It bothers her more that her supervisors think more about the budget than the people that she is trying to help. These are not just data. They represent human beings with feelings! Have they no sense of compassion?

The problem of self-sovereignty is as old as the human race. We want to control our lives. Often this then extends itself to our belief that we have the right to control others especially when they are a factor in effecting our circumstances. We are comfortable in our routine of things until we perceive a threat to our security or lifestyle. If we are confronted with change that threatens our control, we usually react in anger. King Saul felt that as king he should be able to control everything. He became angry with his son, Jonathan, when he couldn't control his friendship with David. During a discussion of this friendship, of which Saul disapproved, Saul became so angry that he tried to kill Jonathan, the "son of a perverse, rebellious woman." This would supposedly have re-establish Saul's control. (1 Samuel 20:30 - 33).

I, too, was angered when I was faced with losing control. My oldest daughter, Joan, had completed two years of college at the University of North Alabama while living at home. We have always been a close family. Although my son was in the air force, Joan would be the first one to leave home by choice. She decided to go to Bethany Nazarene College in Bethany, Oklahoma, a distance of 650 miles from home. All the arrangements had been made. She was admitted to the school, had been assigned a room in the dormitory and told when she should arrive on campus. We packed and made the trip. When we arrived, we found that there was no room in the dormitory reserved for her. As the day and the confusion progressed, so did my anger. I had always been "daddy fix-it." I was about to suggest that Joan get back into the car and we would go back to where I could take care of her. It seemed at that point that my heavenly Father whispered to my heart, "I can take it from here!" Reluctantly, I turned the care of my daughter over to Him and my anger assuaged. I have never been sorry.

Jesus became angry when people showed a lack of compassion for the weak and hurting. For example, He became angry when the Pharisees thought more of their "precious rules" than they did about a suffering person. Jesus called to a man with a "withered hand" and ask him to stand up and come forward in front of all the people. Then He asked the Pharisees if it was lawful to heal on the Sabbath. When they didn't respond, He looked at them with anger and then healed the suffering man — even on the Sabbath! (Mark 3:5). It helps Isabelle to know that Jesus was angry at people who showed no compassion.

When the one hurting is someone I love, I become angry if someone fails to show concern. I became very angry on an occasion when Hattie required an ambulance to take her to the hospital in Birmingham. I called the local ambulance service and they refused to take her to Birmingham unless they took her to a local hospital to see "her physician." When I explained that her physician had moved to Colorado and her only doctor was now in Birmingham, they refused to transport her. I felt like they lacked compassion and refused to try to understand the situation. My secretary sensed my anger, learned the cause, and promptly persuaded an ambulance service from another county to provide the necessary transportation. Even some of my students tried to find a solution to the problem. My anger was transformed into gratitude by the compassion of others. The local ambulance company may lack compassion, but many of those who knew the situation did what they could to solve the problem.

A second time that Hattie required an ambulance to transport her to Birmingham, the ambulance service in the neighboring county refused. However, they gave me the reason: "We are partially supported by county tax money. Since you are from another county, we are afraid that while we are transporting your wife to Birmingham someone who has paid taxes in this county might need our ambulance service. At this time, we only have one ambulance available." With that explanation, I accepted their refusal without anger, but with some frustration. It turned out that the doctor in Birmingham sent an ambulance for my wife and the problem was solved. It seems to me that sometimes our anger is based on insufficient information. What seemed like lack of compassion may have been that the local service was simply abiding by the regulations specified in their contract.

Anger, instead of being a monster that infects you, sometimes can be used to help you. I learned a lot from my late wife. She used the energy that came from her anger to help fight her disease. Anger fueled Hattie's courage and helped her fight for her life. She became angry at her cancer and that enabled her to fight the disease so valiantly. The control of her life was threatened and she would not submit without a fight. After her first regimen of radiation treatments, she returned to her job even when she was so weak that she had to support herself by bracing against the wall in order to get to her desk without falling.

In the latter stages of her illness, she became so weak that she could hardly get out of bed. I purchased a walker for her, but she despised it. She would carry the walker and "run" as far as she could and then lean on it to rest. She was "fightin' angry" at the disease that had so weakened her body.

After the surgery mentioned above, I asked if chemotherapy would be necessary. The surgeon replied, "That recommendation will come from Dr. Blank (not his real name)." When we met with Dr. Blank, he was rushed and assertive. He had made up his mind to give Hattie chemotherapy. We were not consulted. I believe that his aggressive style came from his attitude toward cancer. He personally directed Hattie's treatments for a while and then declared her case "uninteresting" and turned it over to a fellow. I became angry with the doctors that would not listen. When Hattie would go over her list of questions or tell them of the side-effects of her treatment, they would not believe any of the side effects except the ones they had prejudged to be expected. If Hattie or I would make a remark that could be taken as criticism, they would immediately become defensive. The doctors would deny that any pain or neuropathy could be related to what they had done. One time when she complained of double-vision. The fellow finally persuaded Dr. Blank that Hattie might be "interesting" again. He came into the room, looked into her eyes and said in surprise, "You do have double vision!" (Well, Dah!) By that time, the side-effects had produced permanent damage. Dr. Blank's attitude changed. He seemed really sorry that he had not paid more attention.

On another occasion when she suffered a partial paralysis of her arm, the surgeon had overslept that morning and was late entering the Operating Room. He evidently rushed because he acted irritated. Hattie felt something snap during a minor opera-tion which he performed. When Hattie confronted him about the partial paralysis, he said, "Oh, there are lots of nerves in the shoulder and maybe I did damage one of them, but the paralysis is not due to that." It was obvious that the doctors were not in control. And to think that we had trusted them!

The most important lesson that I learned from Hattie was how to solve the anger problem permanently. When her cancer occurred the final time, we returned to Birmingham. She was told by a doctor, that didn't want to be quoted, that it was his opinion that the new cancer probably was a result of the effects of chemotherapy. Here we were dealing with Dr. Blank again. He seemed humble. His wife had been diagnosed as having cancer. From that experience, he was made aware that his patients were people. Now he seemed to listen more carefully to what Hattie had to say. Hattie had become a person with a dreadful disease and was no longer an "interesting" or "uninteresting" case. Although Hattie was aware of the misery that Dr. Blank had caused and real-ized that she would probably die from the results of his decision, she forgave him. She said, "He just made a bad value judgment."

About midway through the second regimen of chemother-apy, Dr. Blank left the clinic for another position. The final time that Hattie saw him, she said, "Thanks for all that you tried to do." He turned and looked at her thinking that she was being sarcastic, but when he saw that she was sincere, he was speechless. In this day of malpractice suits, evidently he was not accustomed to being forgiven. Forgiveness had released any anger that Hattie might have felt toward those who caused her to lose her life while trying to save it.

Toward the end of Hattie's life, she was treated hatefully by the hospital staff. For example, her neuropathy had progressed to the point that she could not empty her bladder. One morning she was in such pain that she begged the nurse to catheterize her. The nurse responded: "Do it yourself." By this time, Hattie was so weak that she could not even sit up in bed much less catheterize herself. . In a couple of days, Dr. Krim signed her discharge papers. While I went for the car, the nurses got her up and into a wheelchair. She promptly passed out. Even then, when she revived, they brought her down and helped me lay her in the back seat of my car. However she didn't waste her energy in anger. A couple of weeks later, she was placed in the CCU in the same hospital and had a "code blue." When she came back to consciousness, she was on a respirator and had all the tubes to take care of her body functions. One day when my son and I went in to see her during visiting hours, she said, "Guess who came to see me? Dr.Krim. He seemed surprised that I was so ill!" From her expression it was obvious to us that she had forgiven him.

When Hattie died, my first reaction was disbelief. Anger came several months later. This time, it was not directed toward God, Hattie, or the doctors. Mine was a generalized anger vaguely directed toward my limitations. I felt as though I had failed. My generalized anger manifested itself in my impatience. Normally, I am quite rational while I am driving. If someone cuts in front of me, I back off. If there is a slow driver in the fast lane, I try to act rationally. When my anger was at its peak, I drove irrationally. If someone cut me off, I would flash my lights and then tailgate him. I was a danger to myself and to others. I was frustrated at my loss of something I thought that I was entitled to and wanted to find some means of expression to let me feel that I was still in charge. Then the lesson that I learned from Hattie about forgiveness began to work for me. When I was irritated by the way someone was driving I forgave him or her. Then I could act rather than react.

Isabelle realized that her depression was due in part from the anger that was caused by her job situation. First, she forgave those responsible but she still refused to do anything unethical or illegal. Then she applied for and received a transfer. In the new department, her supervisor is more honorable. He also respects her judgment. Her colleagues work with her as she is able to develop them into a team. Under these new circumstances, after her treatment for clinical depression, she is beginning to move out of the canyon. Instead of becoming a victim of anger, she is moving past the monster by forgiveness and positive action.

Anger that is unresolved by forgiveness can fester into an uncontrollable hatred that demands revenge. In real life, often revenge is used as an alternative to forgiveness. Absalom dealt with his sister's disgrace in this manner. Amnon, Absalom's half-brother, became infatuated with Absalom's sister, Tamar. Amnon fantasized until he became morbid. One of his cousins suggested a scheme whereby he could satisfy his lust. The scheme was implemented and Amnon violated Tamar. Immediately, he hated her with a passion and sent her away humiliated. Absalom told Tamar that he would take care of the matter and fixed a room in his house where she could live in seclusion. Absalom acted as though nothing had happened but inside his anger was developing into a plot for revenge. Two years later, he held a celebration of sheep shearing and invited all the king's sons. Amnon came with all the rest. After he became drunk, Absalom gave a sign to his servants and they killed Amnon. However, Absalom had to flee the country to save his life. Usually "sweet revenge" is bitter after it is accomplished. (2 Samuel 13).

I recently visited my daughter in Oklahoma. While I was there, we went to the memorial commemorating the dead in the

Alfred P. Murrah Federal Building blast. At 9:00 a.m. on April 19, 1995, Timothy McVeigh pulled his rental truck into the curved driveway in front of the building and left it. Two minutes later, it exploded and destroyed a large portion of the building and damaged much of the surrounding area. As a result 169 people lost their lives. Why? It is reported that he was angry at the way the Branch Davidian standoff was handled in Waco, Texas two years earlier. After brooding, his anger turned into a deadly plot for revenge against the federal government. Although this hatred infected only a couple of other men, sometimes hatred can spread to a whole network of people. For example, Asama bin Ladin and his al Qaeda network of terrorists.

Now that we have dispensed with anger by forgiveness, perhaps we can use forgiveness in dealing with other problems. Being "hurt" is a common experience. The "hurt" might be slight or serious, imagined or real, accidental or intentional, but it must be dealt with. Forgiveness is effective in dealing with "hurt." An alternative to forgiving is resentment and self-pity. Resentment is reliving the hurt again and again. It simply reinforces the pain. The more we replay the incident that caused us hurt, the more that bitterness grows in our selves. We develop the feeling that we have the right to hold a grudge. Self-pity becomes an all consuming lifestyle. Self-pity eventually leads to depression. Then we tend to push people away and put up a shield so that we won't be hurt any further. This isolation reinforces the idea that we deserved the hurt and so must wallow in it. Depression follows. This only compounds the problem.

It is a natural tendency to resist forgiving someone who has hurt us. By withholding forgiveness, we imagine that we are punishing the person who hurt us. We rationalize that we will withhold forgiveness until he has obviously "learned his lesson." In so doing, we feel a sense of power over or superiority to the offender. However, often the offender couldn't care less, doesn't realize that he has a lesson to learn or is unaware that you have not forgiven him.

Forgiveness is sometimes misunderstood. Some confuse forgiveness with pardon. Pardon is a judicial term. It refers to the dismissal of the penalty for the wrong done. It is granted by a superior who has the authority to declare that the offender is not required to suffer the penalty for his offense.

Others confuse forgiveness with reconciliation. It opens the door to reconciliation, but reconciliation is a two-party affair. I may forgive someone, but if they will not accept my forgiveness nor forgive me and allow me back into their good graces, then reconciliation cannot occur. Usually, reconciliation requires a change in behavior on the part of the one or both of the parties concerned.

Some think of forgiveness as condoning or excusing a wrongful act — ignoring the offense. In considering the incident of Hattie and Dr. Blank, I notice that both the forgiver and the forgiven were well aware of the offense. In talking with Hattie, I realized that she faced up to the problem that the doctor had caused her. By his changed attitude, the doctor acknowledged that he had been wrong. Forgiveness never avoids facing the offense.

While teaching physics at the University of North Alabama, I find that the students didn't mind my weekly quizzes, but they fear my comprehensive exams. One student, a very good student, missed the midterm exam. He came in the next day and told me that he missed the exam because he was afraid. I told him that I appreciated his honesty and forgave him but I didn't forget about it. It would not have been fair to the other students to give him a grade based on his average, ignore the exam altogether, or administer the same test that the other students had taken. So, although I forgave him and thus did not give him an automatic "zero," I gave him another exam.

There are those that think that we show love, caring and compassion by condoning certain wrongs because of who committed them. True love is not blind. The parent that allows his child to continue to disobey is not being a loving and forgiving parent, but is doing the child a disservice. It is never a matter of "Oh, it was nothing!" I take my cue from God's attitude toward sin.

An act of sin is an offense against God. God will forgive confessed sin in a manner that is just. (1 John1:9). When Adam and Eve sinned, they were driven from the presence of God. God could not ignore the fact of their disobedience. God hated the fact that the primeval pair had not chosen to trust Him, but in His holiness and justice, He could not ignore the fact. So in order to forgive, God made a decision to send His "only begotten" Son into the world. When Jesus came, he faced sin and the results of sin head on. He accepted rejection by the most religious people of the day. Some of them were the ultimate in orthodoxy. He recognized that their rejection was a result of sin. His painful death on the cross, in the final analysis, was because of the sin of Adam and Eve and everyone since. Only after he had experienced the ultimate penalty for sin, separation from His Father, could He pray when he was dying, "Father, forgive them."(Luke 23:34).

Forgiveness is an internal response to some "hurt" which involves the mind, emotions, and attitudes toward the person who did you the wrong. The first step in forgiveness is to face up to the offense. Be specific. If necessary for clarification sake, write it down. Consider the action that caused you "hurt" and try to decide why that action irritated you so. If you recognize that the offense reminded you of something in your past that left an emotional scar it will be easier to put the offense in proper perspective.

While Jesus was on earth, He taught us that in order to be forgiven, we must be forgiving. In the prayer that He gave His disciples, He taught them to pray: "Forgive us our debts as we forgive our debtors." (Matthew 6:12). Later He emphasized this truth by use of a parable that helps bring offenses against us into the proper perspective.

It seems that a certain king was not a very cautious financier and loaned one of his subjects the equivalent of billions of dollars. The day of reckoning came and of course the man was not able to pay. The king demanded payment, but the man asked for more time and he would pay the debt in full. The king demanded that

the man and his family be sold into slavery and all of their possessions sold and the money applied to the debt. The man begged for
mercy. The king, not being fooled, knew that it would be impossible for the subject to pay the entire amount and so instead of
prolonging the agony, the king forgave his subject the debt.

With great relief, the man went out of the court. On his way
home, he remembered that one of his friends had borrowed one
hundred denarii. (This represented about four month's wages for
the ordinary working man.) His friend promised to pay, but the
man started choking him and finally decided to call in the law and
had his friend thrust into jail.

When the king heard about this unforgiving behavior, he rein-
stated the debt and demanded that the debtor be tortured until the
debt was paid. Jesus then said, "So likewise shall my heavenly
Father do also unto you, if you from your hearts forgive not
everyone his brother their trespasses." (Matthew 18:23 - 35).

Once the "hurt" is clearly seen in the proper perspective, the
next step is to decide to forgive the offender. This is something
that you do for yourself. It is an act of will. Sometimes you need
to say it aloud. "As an act of my will, I hereby forgive Dr. Blank
for not listening to me and therefore allowing the chemotherapy
to do irreparable damage." Probably your emotions will not
follow immediately. You may feel nothing different.

At this point, ask God to help you. We have a right to ask for
God's help in this because He has commanded us to develop a
forgiving attitude. Peter was worried about forgiving "his brother
who had sinned against him." He wondered how much patience
he should have with a repeat offender. Perhaps the perfect number
should be seven times to forgive "his brother." Jesus said, "Not
so, but seventy times seven!" In other words, develop a habit of
forgiving. If that is God's command for you, then He will give
you the grace and strength to obey His command.

David developed a habit of forgiveness. When he was first
provoked by his brother, Eliab, he essentially ignored him. There
was no positive action there. (1 Samuel 17:28 - 30). Later, when

Saul sought to kill him and David had to live a vagabond life, David developed a forgiving spirit because he knew that Saul was "God's Anointed." At least twice, David had an opportunity to kill Saul, but refused. (1 Samuel 24, and 26). Even though he let Saul know what he had done, Saul's feeling of guilt was only temporary and then he would take up his pursuit of David again. David kept on forgiving Saul in spite of the difficulties that he and his men had to face. Thus, by the time of the "Absalom incident," (1 Samuel 18:5-12). David had developed a habit of forgiving. Thus he could tell Joab to deal gently with his son. When the news came of Absalom's death, David wept partially, I believe, because there could be no reconciliation.

The final step in the forgiveness process it to release the hurt. The easiest way to do that is to release it to God. When doing something that is somewhat abstract, many of us are helped by acting it out symbolically. For example, if you have written the details of the hurt on paper, offer it as a "burnt offering" to God. If you haven't written it down, imagine that you are taking it out of your heart with your hand, and then open your hands with the palms up while you say, "God, I am giving this hurt to You and ask that You will help me not to take it back."

I am not artistic. When I was in college, one of the other members in the Honor Society was in charge of some promotion that we were sponsoring. She asked me to make some posters. I spent hours (that I really couldn't spare) doing the best that I could. I admit that the posters looked crude and rather "thrown together." She became very angry with me and wouldn't listen to my explanation. The following year, her sister came to school as a freshman. I was attracted to her and asked her for a date. She said, "I'll have to think about it." What she really meant was, "I'll have to ask my older sister." She turned me down. When I found out the reason, I was "hurt." What should I do? I had some influence on campus and could probably cause her older sister some grief. But I decided to forgive her. It wasn't easy and we never did become close friends. In retrospect, she really did me a favor.

When I learned more about her sister, I am glad that I didn't get entangled with her! She wasn't a bad girl, it is just that she and I would never have been compatible.

God, through Jesus, has given us a pattern for forgiving. He will give us strength to make it a way of life. It is working for us as we learn together.

CHAPTER 16

LIFE UNDER A CLOUD

Summary: Clouds are important to our life's journey. Some of the clouds considered are: the cloud of loss and subsequent change, the cloud of divine guidance, the cloud of protection from danger — seen and unseen, the cloud that protects us from seeing the future, the cloud of delays and the cloud of revelation. If we follow the cloud, at the end of the journey, we will live in the land of cloudless day.

"Here we are on the mesa again, but things look different. Where is the sunshine?"

"We are under a cloud."

"You're right. I wonder if that is necessarily a bad thing? Anyway, it's good to be back to a measure of mental health again."

Looking around, clouds have come into everyone's life. But then, without a cloud, there would be no rain and therefore, life would be a desert. Even so, usually I prefer to live in the sunshine. Is there any other benefit that can come from living under a cloud? If you are a Christian facing a cloud, you can encourage yourself with the song writer who declares that God moves in a mysterious way to perform His wonders. The dreadful, threatening clouds actually are heavy with the mercy and grace of God.

There are many kinds of clouds. There is the cloud of seeing a loved one gradually being taken from you by some debilitating disease. Jim and Susie are still living under that cloud. They are on the mesa of mental health again because they see Arthur as a normal teenager who has a positive outlook on life. But the cloud still hangs over. Just recently Arthur's muscular dystrophy has caused severe scoliosis. This is putting pressure on his heart and left lung and has become life-threatening. The doctors are going to put two stainless Steel rods in his back and fasten them to Arthur's spine. If successful, this will straighten out his back enough to provide relief. Jim and Susie are optimistic. Arthur is still upbeat. They believe that God's grace is sufficient.

There is the cloud of a broken relationship. Sometimes this is accompanied with a sense of futility and failure. Michelle has experienced this. Having been driven from her home by her husband, Andy, she has been struggling with the lack of direction in her life. But the cloud has proven to be an opportunity for God to reveal His grace. Because of her faith she lost her home. Now she is a developing better relationship with her father, mother and siblings. They have a "manufactured home" where she can live rent-free until something else develops. They encourage her by telling her that she did the only thing that she could under the circumstances. She is able to do laundry for others to make a little money for food. Although the cloud still looks ominous, her faith in God has revived and she is optimistic about the future.

There is the cloud of fear due to change. Larry's life situation has changed due to a broken relationship. While he was in the canyon, he had hoped for reconciliation. Now he is mentally healthy again because he has closure. He has faced the situation and realized that Cynthia is determined not to return. Now he is alone, but is ready to face the future. He has a good job, a good church, reliable friends and hope. He believes that God has a plan for his future.

Isabelle has never adjusted well to change. The cloud of

change has hung heavy over her. Because of the situation in her job, she was forced to consider finding another work situation or slip back into depression. As related in a previous chapter (chapter 15) she applied for and received a transfer. She now has cooperative colleagues and a supportive supervisor who recognizes her training and skills. She has also found a church where a small group has interests similar to hers. She is getting spiritual help from attending these meetings and feels safe in sharing her problems with individuals in the group. She is dating a fine Christian young man who lives by a similar value system as she.

There are also other clouds. There is the cloud of protection from dangers seen and unseen, real and imagined — an unrevealed future so that we are not overwhelmed.

"What about the cloud of guidance and trust — a life secure in the hands of a loving heavenly Father Who will guide you into the path of self-fulfillment?"

"Yes, and consider the cloud of waiting — standing still and seeing the redeeming power of God."

"There is also the cloud of revelation, the glory of the Lord — a better grasp, a deepening insight into the true nature of things."

Wow! Clouds are not all bad. This cloud rolling in seems to be the cloud of loss and subsequent change. It covered the Children of Israel a long time ago. The Children of Israel had complained bitterly about the cruelty of the Egyptian slave masters and prayed continually for deliverance. Upon deliverance, there was a sense of loss. Their lifestyle was interrupted. Their security was removed. They were free and they were not sure that they liked it. There is something comfortable about the familiar, the routine, the expected. In their life under a cloud, they had to trust God. They didn't know where their next meal was coming from. They didn't know where they would spent the night. They didn't know what they would be doing tomorrow. But there was no going back.

I've been here before. Have you? When I left home to attend Eastern Nazarene College at age sixteen, I was fully aware that there could be no return. Oh, my parents would have allowed me to return home, but it would never be the same. Once I left home, it was as though I was making a statement — "From here on, I am taking responsibility for my own decisions." It was frightening. I had never ridden on any public transportation or been away from home over night except with my parents. I had never taken a shower — just a bath in a number two washtub. A whole new world lay in front of me. I was afraid. There was a cloud that obscured the future and so I had to trust God for His guidance.

When Hattie died, my life changed. She had cooked, cleaned house, did the laundry, kept things going. Now, I have the responsibility of seeing that these things are taken care of. But what I miss most is her companionship. The house seems especially empty at night. It is surprising how many new unfamiliar sounds occur in the familiar house when you are there by yourself. But there is the trustworthy pillar of cloud to guide me through my sorrow.

When we saw Sarah this morning, her eyes were shining.

"What's up, Sarah?"

"I got a job. It is a temporary job in a bakery. I am learning to frost cupcakes with a swish of the spatula and to decorate a sheet cake with flowers and borders. It is good to have a job again. At the same time, Mike found a job. Because of his age, he is limited in what he can do, but already I can see him beginning to take responsibility. I have a notion that when school starts his grades will improve."

"But Sarah, your job is only temporary and it probably doesn't pay as well as your other job."

"That is true. It pays considerably less. But remember, the cost of my housing is much less than it was. This job came along in time for me to pay my part of the rent so that I will not be a burden on the other widow. I believe that even though this job is temporary, it will last until God brings the permanent solution to my financial difficulties into my life. I will trust and follow the God Who is sometimes hidden in the cloud."

Guided by a cloud? How strange, but God sometimes uses

that means. The cloud of guidance often does things that we don't understand. When Pharaoh let the Children of Israel go it would make sense that they would travel the well known route from Egypt to Canaan directly. There were two things wrong with this — They were not ready to enter the Promised Land, and God promised Moses that, as a sign, He would bring the Children of Israel out of Egypt to worship Him in "this mountain." There are times that we must travel in the dark. Or to put it another way, we cannot see around the bend in the road.

God had led me to teach physics at a university in Florence, Alabama. The physics professor had left suddenly about a week before the Fall semester. The Head of the Department asked me if I could teach physics for him. I had enough to teach the beginning course, and agreed to that. I found a university in Huntsville, about seventy miles away, that had physics classes at night. I enrolled and worked off an undergraduate major in physics. I taught full-time at Florence and went to school at night in Huntsville. Then I started to take graduate classes in physics, but couldn't seem to get anything but "B"s even though I had made "A"s in the undergraduate program. Then came the bomb. I made a "C" in Quantum Mechanics and landed on academic probation. I was devastated. I had always prided myself in being a good student and had never been in academic trouble before through three years of graduate work in Nazarene Theological Seminary and a master's degree at the University of North Carolina. Also, my undergraduate work in physics was excellent. But now — Academic Probation?

God tried to soften the blow and assure me that He was guiding me. A few months before this happened, a friend of mine had sent me some LP records. Among the records was one by some Scottish singers that sang a cappella. Among the songs was a song that captured my attention. After playing it many times, I was able to learn the words. The message was that we need not fear the "bend in the road," but we can travel in confidence and hope. The road is safe because Jesus has traveled the road before us and promises to guide our every step. As I prayed through my humiliation and disappointment, the haunting refrain of this song kept coming back to me. "The bend in the road" — Is this just a bend in the road? Is God directing me to change directions? Am I through with physics? I still have my teaching job.

I dropped the course that I had enrolled in and decided to wait before the Lord. The next semester, I enrolled in an advanced optics course. When I bought the textbook, I wondered if this was the *end* of the road instead of the *bend* in the road. The book was one that says: "It can be shown that . . ." and sure enough with two or three pages of math it can be shown that. Throughout the course of the semester there were little signs to encourage me. A major part of the grade was based on an oral report. I was accustomed to teaching and so with the visual aids I made, the report went well. He then announced that the final exam would be oral. I felt confident because I felt that I could do well one-on-one with the professor. The time for the exam came and I was prepared. The Lord gave me insight into the material and when the exam was over the professor said, "Mr. Allison, you know more optics than anyone in the class." Whether that was true or not, I was happy to have the probation removed. I then moved to the Tuscaloosa campus.

Another time that I needed hindsight to see the guidance of a cloud happened after my family and I had been in Tuscaloosa for three years. I was on a leave of absence from the University of North Alabama working on my doctor's degree. The president of the university wrote that my leave could not be extended beyond the next Fall semester. After negotiating another contract, I agreed to return even though I had not completed my work for the Ph.D. It was a frustrating time. However, when I returned to the University of North Alabama as I had promised, I found that the president had retired and there was a new president beginning that semester. Also, the job market had collapsed for physicists and I would have had a tough time finding other employment.

When we arrived in Florence, Hattie was contacted to see if

she would work at TVA. Rather reluctantly, she agreed. Part of the employment procedure included a physical exam with a chest x-ray. This proved to be providential because that was the x-ray that was needed to show the health insurance company that the cancer was not a "pre-existing condition."

Another cloud that conceals blessings is the cloud of protection from danger — seen and unseen. The Children of Israel were trapped. God had led them into a dead-end situation. When Pharaoh told them to leave, they headed south. When they came to the main route to Canaan, they crossed it and continued south. It looked like God had made a mistake but He knew that they were not ready to engage in combat at the garrison on the border. They were turned back from going north of the sea. Finally, they camped by the sea and suddenly realized that the Egyptian army was pursuing them. (Exodus 14). It was then that the cloud that had been leading them went around behind them and formed a barrier between the them and the Egyptians. To Israel it was a cloud of fire and served as a source of illumination but to the Egyptians, it was a cloud of darkness and confusion. God provided a route through the sea on dry land and the cloud provided cover for the Israelites. When the Egyptians tried to follow, their chariots bogged down and in the confusion of the cloud they lost their way. Then the waters were restored to their normal position. It caught the Egyptians and they were drowned.

The summer I turned sixteen, I worked with my father as a carpenter. (My father was a bi-vocational minister.) I was malnourished and constantly tired. Can God use this cloud in any way? One day my father and I were working on a way to support a house while we put new sills under it. I was holding a four by four while my father was hammering it into place. Since I was tired, I had leaned my head over against the wall. Shortly after that, my father took a mighty swing with his hammer but missed the timber and the hammer flew past me over my right shoulder. If I had been standing up straight, the hammer head would have hit me squarely in the middle of my forehead. I might have been killed, but more probably I would have suffered serious brain damage.

Clouds also hide things, protecting us from seeing the future. The cloud moved ahead of the Children of Israel a little at a time. If they had known what lay ahead, they might have refused to leave Egypt. As it was, they constantly complained. There is no water. The drinking water is bitter. There is nothing to eat. "Would to God we had died by the hand of the Lord in the land of Egypt, when we sat by the flesh pots, when we ate bread to the full; for you have brought us forth into this wilderness to kill this whole assembly with hunger." (Exodus 16:3). I hate this "manna." Why can't we have some meat? And the Lord showed His glory in a cloud. (Exodus 16:10). He promised and provided meat. No matter what, the people continued to complain. Had God lifted the cloud and shown them what lie ahead, they would have rebelled more vigorously than they did.

When Hattie became hoarse and nothing seemed to help, God protected us by the cloud of the unrevealed future. If we had been allowed to see the next thirteen years, we could not have taken it. The diagnosis — cancer. Four operations to try to determine what kind of cancer it was, exploratory surgery, surgery to remove as much of the cancer as possible, radiation therapy, trying to maintain my teaching job and taking care of Hattie and the children. Decisions, decisions. Just to remember it all nearly overwhelms me. Yet, there were good things — compassionate friends and students, prayers from a host of people, a place to stay near the hospital, children who loved us and cared, colleagues who helped share the load, some meals from people of the church and Hattie's unusual stamina. Looking back on it, being led one step at a time was a blessing.

Generally, we Americans are an impatient people. The word "wait" is not in our vocabulary. However, there are times that God indicates that we need to wait. The Children of Israel had to learn to wait. The cloud, representing the presence of the Lord, would direct them when to move and when to stay put. "And when the cloud was taken up from the tabernacle, then after that the children of Israel journeyed: and in the place where the cloud abode, there the children of Israel pitched their tents. At the commandment of the Lord the children of Israel journeyed, and at the commandment of the Lord they pitched; as long as the cloud abode upon the tabernacle, they rested in their tents. And when the cloud tarried long upon the tabernacle many days, then the children of Israel kept the charge of the Lord, and journeyed not." (Numbers 9:17 - 19). This implicit trust in the erratic behavior of the cloud must have frustrated some of the eggheads of the group. They tried to make sense out of the stopping and going. The waiting must have been especially baffling to some of them. "Let's see if we can find a reason for this delay." I am usually impatient with delays whether they are caused by a cloud of not.

I have a tendency to try to "figure things out." Clouds frustrate that. Sometimes in retrospect, I can see what the Lord had in mind. When I moved to Versailles, Kentucky, I thought that I would continue my graduate work at the University of Kentucky. I could go to summer sessions and perhaps work something out to take a few classes during the school year. I had planned to pursue a degree in mathematics. I signed up for a course in differential equations. I *was lost* from "day one." I was confused. I prayed and studied my choices. I decided to drop out of summer session rather than continue in my frustration. In other words, I decided to put my education on hold — to wait. A couple of years later, the Lord opened the door for me to move. (The cloud lifted and it was time to move on!) The Lord also led me into the field of physics. When it came time for me to take my differential equations which I needed to use in physics, I *understood* it from "day one." I was top man in the class. When God said, "Wait," in Kentucky, He was leading me into physics rather than mathematics.

There are also times that a cloud provides me with an insight — a revelation. I see that in the record of the Children of Israel's biblical story. Three months after the Children of Israel left Egypt; they came to "the mountain of the Lord." These had been difficult months with a considerable amount of complaining. Now they were at the place that Moses said that they would meet God. God wanted to make a covenant with them. He said to Moses, "Lo, I come unto you in a thick cloud, that the people may hear when I speak with you and believe you for ever." (Exodus 19:9). When the people had consecrated themselves and approached the mountain — they were forbidden to touch the mountain — there appeared a "thick cloud" that obscured the top of the mountain. There was lightning, thunder, smoke, earthquake and confusion among the Children of Israel. It was a dreadful experience. Even Moses was afraid — "And so terrible was the sight, that Moses said, 'I exceedingly fear and quake.'" (Hebrews 12:21). But out of that experience came a new sense of who God is.

About a month before Hattie died, she was so weak that she could not get out of bed. Our oldest daughter took her vacation to come and be with us for a week. During that time, she washed Hattie's hair and did some other things that made her mother feel more like a real person again. But, there was another difference. It is hard to put my finger on, but she seemed to have an aura of love about her that she did not have before. When she was working as a travel clerk, she was a "whistle-blower." It infected her spirit with a critical attitude about other things as well. Now this was entirely gone. God had penetrated her personality with a new sense of His Presence. The ominous cloud of death turned out to be a cloud of revelation.

After the Children of Israel passed over the Jordan into the "Promised Land," the manna ceased and it is presumed that the cloud lifted. Moses was dead and Joshua had been given the responsibility for leading the people in the conquest of Canaan. In one sense of the word, they had arrived. The journey was over.

Hattie died. She left this world for her eternal home. Various clouds had been a part of her life. She was led from Hominy, Oklahoma to Kansas City, Missouri. She was led to worship at the First Church of the Nazarene, to sing in the choir, to work in the Nazarene Publishing House, to meet and marry me, to be a helpmate as we served pastorates in Pennsylvania, Vermont,

North Carolina and Kentucky, give birth to our children, to work at various jobs to help with the finances, to finally endure the ravages of cancer and to go home. Now she dwells in the land of cloudless day.

ENDNOTES

1. Doctor of Philosophy — A degree that usually takes at least three years as a full-time student after four years of full-time undergraduate college work. The requirements differ from one school to another. Many require reading ability in two foreign languages. Sometime during the first year there is a Preliminary Exam to test your knowledge of the field. Your course is then set to prepare you for your Comprehensive Exams that consist of written and oral exams to test your comprehension of the entire field — in Isabelle's case of psychology. In the meantime, you and your advisor decide on a research project. The goal is to discover something and publish it before someone else publishes the information. The description of your discovery is written up in a book-length paper called a "dissertation." After the dissertation is approved by a committee of scholars, it must be defended in a session where you make an oral presentation followed by a period of questioning. If the committee is convinced that you are thoroughly familiar with the subject and have contributed significant new knowledge to the field, you publish your findings in a professional journal and provide the university library with at least two copies of your dissertation. At this point you are ready to receive your diploma.

2. The "Way of Salvation" is also the way to "be saved." First you must acknowledge that you are a sinner and confess (i.e., take full, personal responsibility for your sinful acts) your sins and ask God to forgive you. (1 John 1:9). Then invite Jesus to come into your heart and ask Him to order your life. (Revelation 3:20). Believe that He does it because He said He would.

APPENDIX

THE CAT

"Thou shalt eat no food
    And thou shalt drink no drink
      After midnight."
      "Thou shalt drink this cup!"
      (A quart of barium 'milkshake'.)
      Gag!
      And yet the insulted physical system
      Is subject to her will.
"Take off your clothes.
      Put on ours."
      Strip of personhood,
      Become a thing.
      Things are easier to manipulate.
      "NO! He can't come with you!"
The path is lonely; the people as impersonal
      As the machine they operate.
      Enter the tunnel head first.
      Could this be death's prelude?
      The x-ray eyes of the CAT
      And its computer brain do their stuff.
      There is an end to this tunnel.
"Permission granted,
      You may return to your loved one."
      A person again!
      Weak, but loving and loved.

THE COBALT TREATMENT

The doctors are professional.
>The nurses are friendly.
>The atmosphere is tense with attention.
>I am placed on a slab.
>Among the murmur of voices from behind the lead
>screen,
>I distinguish the voice of my loved one.
>He is with me.

The room is dark
>Except for the harmless, red laser beams
>Eerie as from another world,
>The world of cold, unforgiving technology.
>Invisible rays penetrate my body,
>Displaying to those behind the lead screen,
>The offending mass invading my spine

The slab moves,
>>My body is marked,
>The stretcher comes,
>Transporting me to a tomb.
>Again I am on a slab,
>Again the room is darkened
>Again the laser beams lend their atmosphere.

The heavy door swings shut,
>The interlock engaged.
>Alone, forsaken by all
>Dear God, do You know I'm here?
>A small red light comes on
>The cobalt sends out its deadly rays,
>Killing my cancer
>And, ultimately, me.

Now the lonely trip is over.
     I return to Professional doctors,
     Friendly nurses,
     And, best of all, my loved one,
     Who holds my hand.
All too soon I will take another lonely trip,
     One from which I will not return
     And even my loved one cannot go with me.
     Dear God, will You go with me?

CHEMO

Drip . . . Drip . . . Drip . . .
Poisoning my system one drop at a time.
Drip . . . Drip . . . Drip . . .
Liquid clock "ticking" away my life.
Will they stop this thing in time?
One hour, two . . .
Still I wait and so does my loved one
My arm flames a warning: POISON ENTERING!
Perhaps if I doze it will forestall my nausea
Three . . . four . . .
The bottles are nearly empty now.
Will I make it home in time?
How many treatments does this one make?
I can't remember.
I do know there will be a last one.
I will make it because my family needs me.
Lord, let me live a little longer for their sake.
My hair falls out.
A "friend" says, "I see you're wearing a wig!"
Lord, help me to be kind.
I retain fluid and run a low-grade fever.
"You look so good!"
"I am dying but 'I look so good'
What a corpse I will make!"
"Lord, give me the patience to love.
Cancer, chemotherapy, pain, nausea, . . .
Lord, give me strength to fight,
But through it all,
May I manifest Your spirit."
(These prayers were graciously answered.)

THE MONITOR

Electronic wonder,
      Messenger of hope.
      Displaying my lover's heart potentials
      In Q-R-S mountains, strong and regular.
We look and we believe.

Days follow days.
      Your message is the same
      Other instruments vary,
      But Q-R-S regular and strong.
Our hope is sustained.

But now even your face is changed.
      Q-R-S too sharp and widely spaced.
      Your message to me is clear:
      "Your wife is dying!"
Should I punch your lights out?

No, You simply display what is sent.
      All too soon your face will be blank.
      Oh emotionless monster,
      See my tears! Don't you care?

Your face is blank — unchanging —
      As dead as my loved one.
      I should have remembered,
      Only humans love.

BLESSING OR CURSE?

Oh love, maker of pain,
> Thou hast strangled my heart
> Weaving my life into the warp and woof of another
> And now she is gone and my life is in shreds.

Oh love, maker of fear,
> Thou hast stolen my heart as a gift to my children
> Wrenching it from me as my teenage daughter is left in
> the hospital
> And raising the specter of cancer and death.

Oh love, maker of hope,
> Thou hast fanned my aspirations into a flame
> Feeding my desire to avenge my sweetheart's death.
> And now do not deceive me — Let me win!

Oh love, guarantor of eternal life,
> Thou hast shown me the nature of God
> Giving me confidence that my sweetheart is with Him.
> And nourishing my faith!

THE DAWN

My wife is dead.
> I fly alone.
> Fog shrouds the earth.
> Darkness shrouds my heart.
The sun faithfully tries to kiss the earth.
> A flash of light! The sun succeeds!
> A farm pond relays the message.
> I wonder!?
Another pond glitters its welcome news,
> Then another, and another, and another,
> Until it is as a thousand stars,
> Twinkling in the distance on the earth below.
My spirit reaches weakly toward God.
> My mind sees: sunlight reflected in water.
> My heart sees: stars on earth.
> My soul feels the tension.
Slowly the fog loses to the sun.
> Slowly my mind accepts the deeper truth,
> And slowly my heart turns to await another day . . .
> With hope.

(This was written on an early morning flight from Oklahoma City to Dallas looking east.)

WHO AM I?

I am a chemical system
        Close-knit families of carbon
        Intermarried to other members of the chemical family.
I am a physical system
        Cooperative neighborhoods of subsystems
        Organized to run smoothly and working happily
        together.
I am a biological system
        A product of genetic-code-driven slaves
        Marvelously manufacturing the right stuff in the right
        amounts.
I am a complex history
        A living record of all my past
        Which filters all my experiences, infusing them with
        meaning.
I am a rational being
        A mind contemplating its own destiny
        Sometimes making sense out of internal and external
        chaos.
I am a volitional being
        A will saddled with the power of choice
        Determining my lot by the pattern of choices that I
        weave.
I am an emotional being
        A temperament moved by emotions light and dark
        Sometimes overwhelmed by the strength of their
        tyranny.
I am a real person
        A united mind, will, and temperament
        Thinking, choosing, and loving, I interact with other
        people.

I am a loving father
    A parent secure in the love of my family
    Laughing together and crying together we grow.
I am a spiritual man
    A child of my heavenly Father
    Creating a link between the physical and spiritual
    realms.

IN MEMORIAM

HATTIE ROBERTS ALLISON
January 6, 1925 — April 23, 1985

To you who taught us the deeper meaning of loyalty by your faith in God which led you to do His will consistently. Your dedication to God prompted you to push yourself to devotion even when your body cried out with fatigue and pain. Your loyalty to God showed itself in your trust of your family, your faithfulness to your church and your dependability at work.

To you who taught us the deeper meaning of honesty by your unswerving dedication to the truth. Your commitment to the One Who said, "I am the Truth," was seen in your ardent search for truth in all your relationships. This honesty before God left no room for hypocrisy.

To you who taught us the deeper meaning of love by your self-giving attitude and your care and concern for others. Your grasp of the meaning of life showed that you believed that the essence of life is love. Your love for God was manifest by your priorities. He was number ONE in your life. As death approached, your love mellowed you so that it seemed that by death God was saying, "You have successfully finished your course. It's time you graduated."

And now you are beyond the reach of pain, fatigue, heartache, and frustration. You are rejoicing this Easter morning with your Risen Lord in your new freedom that allows you to continue to live faithfully, to enjoy new insights into truth, and to love without fear of being misunderstood. In this we rejoice.

102692

Printed i

107798L

102692

9 781597 815062